PRAISE FOR
THRESHOLDS OF THE MIND

"Thresholds of the Mind *is a work of genius. I urge everyone to read,* *use, and benefit from the magnificent breakthrough Bill Harris has made.*"

AL SIEBERT, PH.D.
AUTHOR OF *THE SURVIVOR PERSONALITY*
DIRECTOR OF THE RESILIENCY CENTER

"*In* Thresholds of the Mind, *Bill Harris offers a creative and practical new twist on why we suffer, and how, despite our resistance, we can attain deep happiness and inner peace, regardless of our past or present conditions.* Thresholds of the Mind *will benefit anyone interested in creating dramatic and powerful positive change.*"

JACK CANFIELD, CO-AUTHOR OF THE #1 NEW YORK TIMES
BEST-SELLING *CHICKEN SOUP FOR THE SOUL®* SERIES.

"*In this remarkable post-modern work, transcendence and technology are joined in unique and potent ways. There is much to ponder here as we advance our understanding of the inherent genius of our mind-body systems and the new ways to tap the potential within us all. Harris brings together hitherto divided and distinguished worlds—science and consciousness—to enable the evolution of our species in these most challenging of times.*"

JEAN HOUSTON PH.D
AUTHOR OF 17 BOOKS INCLUDING JUMP TIME, PROTEGE OF ANTHROPOLOGIST MARGARET MEAD, CO-SEMINAR LEADER WITH MYTHOLOGIST JOSEPH CAMPBELL, PAST-PRESIDENT OF THE ASSOCIATION OF HUMANISTIC PSYCHOLOGY, CO-DIRECTOR OF THE FOUNDATION FOR MIND RESEARCH

"*Bill Harris has helped thousands of people reach new heights of awareness, and with this informative book millions more will have the opportunity. For many years Kathlyn and I have taught that the central problem human beings face is what we call the Upper Limits problem—the tendency to settle below the threshold of what is possible to achieve. Bill Harris not only understands this problem, he has created an ingenious technology for breaking through it, With the remarkable Holosync audio technology developed at Centerpointe Research Institute, all of us can now learn to live at a new and higher level of functioning. Do yourself a huge favor by reading Thresholds of the Mind and working with Holosync audio technology."*

GAY HENDRICKS, PH.D.
AUTHOR OF *CONSCIOUS LIVING* AND CO-AUTHOR
(WITH DR. KATHLYN HENDRICKS) OF *CONSCIOUS LOVING*
PRESIDENT, THE HENDRICKS INSTITUTE

"With a loving heart, Bill Harris guides us to the thresholds of the mind. This remarkable book is not only a profound tool for healing. It is also an invitation to explore the mystical interface between technology and the soul."

DAPHNE ROSE KINGMA, AUTHOR OF
THE FUTURE OF LOVE, HEART & SOUL, AND *COMING APART*

"Bill Harris comes from deep personal experience with healing and consciousness. Thresholds of the Mind is truly inspiring and filled with profound wisdom. Holosync is the perfect addition to other growth and spiritual processes."

MARGARET PAUL, PH.D.
AUTHOR/COAUTHOR OF *DO I HAVE TO GIVE UP ME TO BE LOVED BY YOU?, HEALING YOUR ALONENESS, INNER BONDING*,
AND *DO I HAVE TO GIVE UP ME TO BE LOVED BY GOD?*

"Bill Harris has woven a wonderfully understandable tapestry of personal possibility in this useful work. Readers will find the just right road map for their own journey of growth and joy page by page."

BOB DANZIG,
FORMER CEO, HEARST NEWSPAPERS;
AUTHOR OF *ANGEL THREADS, SUCCESS VITAMINS*,
SPEAKER, PROFESSOR

"A very compelling concept...I am quite intrigued with its potential. Bill Harris presents a powerful and provocative program that stands apart from the traditional approaches to self improvement."

"Spirituality deals with the fundamentals of human living, happiness, the elimination of suffering, the discovery of the authentic self, the power of love, the understanding of and control of emotions, even the transformation of one's life. When I read Bill Harris' Thresholds of the Mind, I found an approach to spirituality that was very compatible with all I have been teaching and have found helpful to others seeking a deeper understanding of their lives. This book does not pretend to be spiritual in a religious sense, but fills a void in the teaching of spirituality that is most welcome. I highly recommend it."

"Bill Harris has created something very unusual: the perfect marriage of meditation and science. His elegant explanation of how mental, emotional, and spiritual change happen, how and why we make change so difficult, and how we can get out of the way and just let it happen is nothing short of brilliant. This book is a must for everyone committed to lifetime growth and self-improvement."

"I learned SO much from this book and whole-heartedly recommend you read it too. Wow, I might have titled it, 'Brain Flow & True Happiness: A detailed manual.' Bill Harris has managed to put down on paper both a great scientific explanation of why meditation works and a tantalizing description of the profound benefits of Holosync audio technology, which he's witnessed in thousands and documented over the past 15 years. In a world full of quick-fix offerings that fail us constantly, this book shines as a beacon of real hope. Read it if your search for deep happiness is entirely sincere. Or just read it if you want to know important things about how your brain works."

"Bill Harris's Holosync process and the Centerpointe program perfectly blend the technology of the new millennium with its new spirituality. We are definitely not in Kansas anymore! Thanks, Bill!"

"Thresholds of the Mind is a captivating book that holds your attention and heart throughout its thought-provoking pages. Bill's new book is just the tip of the iceberg of a powerful program that offers a journey worthy of the most ardent student of personal development. I am recommending this book to everyone I know."

"Mr. Harris has clearly passed all of his competition by great distances and with great ease in the development of programs for the use of meditation for personal development. His work is indeed worthy of being clearly identified as both a work of significant genius, and the market leader in the domain of personal development."

THRESHOLDS OF THE MIND

THRESHOLDS OF THE MIND

*Your Personal Roadmap to Success,
Happiness, and Contentment*

Bill Harris

Centerpointe Press
Beaverton, Oregon

Disclaimer

None of the information contained in this book should be construed as a claim or representation that Holosync® audio technology, or any other products, services, or advice of Centerpointe Research Institute are intended for use in the diagnosis, cure, treatment, or prevention of disease or any other medical condition. In dealing with any medical or mental health condition, always consult a physician or mental health professional.

Library of Congress Control Number: 2002092917

ISBN 0-9721780-0-7

Printed in the United States of America. The End® and Holosync® are registered trademarks of Centerpointe Research Institute, Inc. For information write to Centerpointe Research Institute, 1700 NW 167th Place, Suite 220, Beaverton, Oregon 97006.

Design and illustrations by Visual Images Graphic Design

To Janean, who has made my life complete.

LIFE IS LIKE PLAYING A VIOLIN SOLO IN PUBLIC, LEARNING THE
INSTRUMENT AS YOU GO.

—ANONYMOUS

FOR A LONG TIME IT HAD SEEMED TO ME THAT LIFE WAS ABOUT TO
BEGIN—REAL LIFE. BUT THERE WAS ALWAYS SOME OBSTACLE IN THE WAY,
SOMETHING TO BE GOTTEN THROUGH FIRST, SOME UNFINISHED BUSINESS, TIME
STILL TO BE SERVED, A DEBT TO BE PAID. THEN LIFE WOULD BEGIN. AT LAST IT
DAWNED ON ME THAT THESE OBSTACLES WERE MY LIFE.

—ALFRED D. SOUZA

I WOULD RATHER BE ASHES THAN DUST! I WOULD RATHER THAT MY
SPARK SHOULD BURN OUT IN A BRILLIANT BLAZE THAN IT SHOULD BE STIFLED BY
DRY ROT. I WOULD RATHER BE A SUPERB METEOR, EVERY ATOM OF ME IN
MAGNIFICENT GLOW, THAN A SLEEPY AND PERMANENT PLANET. THE PROPER
FUNCTION OF MAN IS TO LIVE, NOT TO EXIST. I SHALL NOT WASTE MY DAYS IN
TRYING TO PROLONG THEM. I SHALL USE MY TIME.

—JACK LONDON

Acknowledgments

I would like to thank the following people who were instrumental in either the creation of Centerpointe Research Institute or in the writing of this book: My dear wife Janean, whose love frees me to create; all the wonderful participants in the Centerpointe program, all over the world, who really want to know who they are and are busy doing something about it; Jean Staehli, who poured over nearly a hundred of my articles and other writings and listened to many hours of me speaking to extract what ended up in this book, and otherwise helped give the book form; my editor, Ken Banks; Beverlee Marks Taub, Ph.D., for helping screw my head on straight; my fantastic staff at Centerpointe, without whom I would be lost; and all the many teachers who over the years have taught me what is really important in life.

Foreword

⑥

When I was young, I often went to prayer meetings on Wednesday night at my local Baptist church. We talked to God—praying for others and confessing our shortcomings. While there was a moment of silence before the prayers began, we never meditated. Later I received a formal theological education that included only one course on prayer, one course on mysticism, and no courses on meditation. In the course on mysticism, I learned that the term "mysticism" referred to "direct experience of God," but that mystical theology was inferior to systematic theology. Since I was a rationalist, at the time, that ended my interest in the mystical path until much later.

In the early seventies, I attended a workshop at the Esalen Institute, in Big Sur, California, led by John Lilly, M.D. Lilly described his research on the 48 levels of consciousness he had induced using his famous float tank experiments. He also informed us that certain physical and mental exercises, which he would demonstrate in the workshop, could produce outcomes similar to the float tank if we would practice them diligently over a long period of time. However, I became intrigued with the float tank, since that seemed less arduous and was quicker, and eventually purchased one and used it for several months. My experiences were pale compared to Lilly's descriptions of his, so I eventually abandoned the project, but my interest in altered states of consciousness had been pricked, and I turned to a study of meditation.

My initial venture into meditation was more academic than experiential—my usual initial approach to a subject. Most of the literature was dry and some of it incomprehensible until I stumbled upon *How To Meditate,* by Lawrence LeShan, a scholar and physician who was interested in the impact of meditation on physical healing. He defined meditation as "doing one thing at a time with your whole being," of bringing one's mental focus to a point and holding it there for increasing lengths of time. He claimed that the effect of such intense and sustained focus was a state of deep relaxation or reduction of stress that contributed to the body's ability to heal itself. This cleared the fog for me regarding the practice of meditation, as well as its potential effects. Later, from Mihaly Csikszentmihalyi's *Flow*, I learned that similar experiences of inner peace, reduced stress and joy were common experiences of ordinary people—factory workers, craftspersons, artists, musicians, gardeners, skilled workers of all sorts, etc.—when they were concentrating entirely on what they were doing. As a writer and lecturer, I identified with that experience and discovered that I had been meditating most of my life—even when I was fishing! I attempted to amplify this experience, off and on, by following LeShan's and Lilly's instructions to just sit, count your breaths, release all interrupting thoughts, and return to the point of focus. But I was not a good student and soon lapsed into my previous state of episodic "flow" experiences while writing or speaking, and was satisfied with that for a time.

In the late 1980s one of my children became interested in Transcendental Meditation. His involvement reactivated my interest in meditation. I followed my usual procedure of reading before experiencing, and became acquainted with the Vedic tradition and philosophy. I learned that meditation is one of the oldest spiritual exercises of humankind. While my son was using it initially as self-medication, he later became interested in it as a spiritual path. After taking advanced courses, he began to talk about the "bliss" state and other levels of consciousness, including the possibility of achieving "cosmic consciousness." This recalled my earlier contact with Lilly's levels of consciousness and those reported by the Christian mystics I had learned about (and dismissed) in my earlier theological studies. I became particularly interested in the claim by meditators and mystics that the aim and outcome of focusing on a point was to achieve a state of "inner silence" wherein one not only encountered, but also participated in, the reality of Divine consciousness. So, I finally got it. The God we sought to invoke in the prayer meetings of my youth was available as a personal experience in moments of meditation deep enough to achieve "deep silence." However, this auspicious experience, according to the meditative traditions, is available only to the hardy few who have the patience and endurance to commit twenty years, more or less, of their lives to the journey. I am not that disciplined!

During my dallying with meditation, many things were happening between the East and the West, namely an invasion of Eastern spiritual traditions into America. Buddhism, Hinduism, Taoism, and Vedic philosophy were not only being taught in graduate schools of comparative religions but also were avidly embraced by the American public, spawning a renaissance of generic spirituality. This challenged Christian traditionalists to revisit their mystical roots and create Christian alternatives to the Eastern invasion. This flurry of activity has produced a "new age" of spirituality, and many, who not more than a decade ago would have shunned spiritual talk and practice, now embrace and advocate it. It has become big business.

At the same time, avowedly non-spiritual professionals, astonished by the ability of seasoned practitioners of meditation to control their autonomic nervous systems, began to study meditation and meditators. Physicians like Herbert Benson, at Harvard, went off to Tibet to study the yogis in their natural habitat, and returned to develop the "relaxation response" and apply the practice to emotional and physical healing, much like LeShan had done earlier. Prayer became a course in Harvard Medical School, and teaching meditation practices became a part of the Harvard medical curriculum.

With the development of scanning devices like PET, scientists began to peer into the brains of yogis, as well as less experienced meditators, to see what happened to their neural processes while in deep meditative states. And many of us have seen those stunning photos of multi-colored brains! This work revealed that, in deep meditative trance—doing one thing at a time with your whole being (a la LeShan)—the two sides of the brain become synchronized, and when that happens one experiences *profound inner peace and happiness and, in addition, an experience of connection to the universe.*

In *Thresholds of the Mind*, Bill Harris asks and answers a challenging and controversial question: *Can technology produce bilateral synchronization and achieve the altered states of consciousness reported by experienced meditators?* With this question, the author entered the controversial discussion about technology and consciousness begun earlier by John Lilly and his float tank experiments. After years of experimentation, Mr. Harris, citing reams of data and personal testimonies of hundreds of participants in his Centerpointe program, asserts and demonstrates that his technology can assist persons in achieving inner states of consciousness that have been reserved since ancient times to devoted, skilled, and life long meditators. In fact, he further asserts that Holosync, the name of his technique of introducing different sound frequencies into the brain through stereo headphones, thus creating a binaural beat, "actually creates even deeper meditative states than are possible through traditional techniques."

Being somewhat undisciplined in my meditative practice, this claim attracted my interest! Coming full circle, starting with my first interest in meditation stimulated by Lilly's experiments with the float tank, I ordered the tapes three years ago and have been using them ever since, with great results. I do not know whether my experience is identical to that of seasoned yogic practitioners, or if I have achieved the traditional state of silence where the interface with the Divine occurs, but I do know that my practice of the Holysync technique has opened doors for me into new levels of awareness. I am aware of deep inner peace, greatly enhanced creativity, and a profound sense of connection to my social and natural context. I live in awe of our cosmic connection, our essential oneness. I hope you, the reader, will taste and see for yourself.

Harville Hendrix, Ph.D.
Author, *Getting the Love You Want: A Guide for Couples*

Introduction

❂

L et me confess right off the bat that I believe we don't have to live lives dominated by emotional dysfunction and suffering—and that *anyone* can live a life of happiness, clarity of mind, and inner peace, regardless of their past or their present condition.

I had no reason to believe this prior to 1985, the year I began using Holosync® audio technology as a meditation tool. At that point in my life, I was 35 years old, and I was miserable. For fifteen years I had tried every approach under the sun in an attempt to get better, with meager and discouraging results. Then, through a series of events I'll relate in this book, everything changed for me. As a result, I started Centerpointe Research Institute as a vehicle for sharing what had worked for me. At the time, I had no idea what a major turning point this was to be in my life—and, as it turned out, in the lives of so many others.

Neither would I have guessed that Centerpointe could grow to the size it is today, with program participants in 172 countries on six continents. When something works, however, it can take on a life of it's own, and despite my initial inexperience at running such a venture, Centerpointe has been a huge success. My guess—and my hope—is that it's best years still lie ahead. I am, as they say, "on a mission."

I am very humbled that I was somehow able to find—and then successfully share—something that has helped so many people. Doing so has made my life satisfying in a way I never would have imagined. In many ways, then, this book is a thank-you to all the people who have helped me to create Centerpointe, and especially all the participants in our program, without whom there would have been no program.

Bookstores are full of self-help books, and more hit the shelves every week. Why should you read this one? First, because this book is about results, not just theory. It's based on the experience of a living laboratory of over 100,000 people, over a thirteen-year period. What this book presents is not pie-in-the-sky, but, rather, the result of the real-world experiences of real people facing the same challenges, and with the same aspirations, as you. If, like these people, you yearn to live a life of great inner peace, happiness, and self-awareness; if you want to heal past emotional traumas and leave behind limitations, whether self-created or imposed upon you; or if you want to explore the most profound depths of who you are and discover your place in this vast universe—this book is for you.

In addition to the experiences of people who have used the Centerpointe program, I've also drawn extensively from discoveries about brain wave patterns and how they relate to meditation and other highly beneficial mental and emotional states, current research in how the human brain adapts, and modern psychological principles.

The Holosync technology we use at Centerpointe provides a precise method of duplicating the brain states experienced by long-time meditators, and, in fact, takes users beyond those states. The benefits of using this technology include deep and lasting contentment and inner peace, a tremendous clarity of mind, deep self-awareness, healing of past emotional traumas, an on-going experience of connection with other people and the rest of the world, and most important, a deep and lasting happiness and joy in being alive. You may have read about similar benefits in books about meditation and personal growth and said to yourself, "Wow! This sounds a lot better than the way I'm living now." You may then have set out to achieve them yourself through traditional meditation or other approaches to personal growth—as I did more than 30 years ago. And although you may have made great strides, if you're like most people, you'll admit that despite all your work, most of these benefits still elude you.

The program I'm going to discuss is different. As hard as it may be to believe, this new approach will leave you saying, "*This* is what I expected when I first tried to meditate. In fact, this is *more* than I expected." The approach we use at Centerpointe Research Institute will do nothing less than allow you to achieve the rewards and benefits of a lifetime of meditation—all of them—in just a few years.

I know this may sound like one of those too-good-to-be-true claims, but I've experienced it myself, taking myself from abject misery and a life that wasn't working to a life of constant happiness and inner peace. Since then, I've seen tens of thousands of other people do the same. What really counts are *results*, and that is what this program delivers.

Happiness, clarity of mind, and inner peace really are available to anyone, no matter what his or her present circumstances. Turn the page and I'll tell you all about it.

CHAPTER 1

⑥

The End is the Beginning of an Adventure

One of the great paradoxes of life is that we must go inward in order to find the road out of ourselves. When we are in touch with our true selves, we free ourselves from the incessant needs, desires, and limitations of our "small selves." As a result, we can get in touch with what lies underneath the crust of our anger and fear and our automatic responses and reactions, and experience ourselves as accepting, resilient, and serene. As a result, we can allow ourselves to open up and become more receptive to both the beauty and challenge of life's larger and more profound dimensions.

Perhaps this inner work is the "absorbing errand" Henry James had in mind. Undertaking the task of discovering who we are, what kind of person we want to be, and what kind of life we want to live may be the most important assignment we ever accept. I'm certain it is the greatest adventure we can ever have.

The problem is how to do it. How are we to proceed on this inward journey? If it were obvious, we'd already be living different lives. Not that there aren't plenty of self-improvement programs and approaches to help us along: you can find advice in every bookstore, on every talk show, and in every self-help seminar. A lot of people are anxious to tell you how to become a better, happier, person. Some of this advice is helpful; some is not. But wading through it to find out which is useful and which isn't can be daunting and time consuming.

In this book I describe a simple program that is clinically proven and personally directed by each individual who uses it. The program is based on technology developed through considerable research on how the human brain changes and evolves in order to better learn new tasks and meet new challenges. I'll also share with you a model of how change happens, at both a physiological and a psychological level. Once you understand this change model, you will be able to see more clearly what is really going on during times of upheaval or emotional imbalance in your life. Understanding the mechanism behind frustration, anxiety, and other upsetting mental and emotional states helps you move through them instead of getting stuck in them. These states then become springboards to tremendous positive change instead of just troubling events in an on-going stream of upsets and personal dramas.

The program we offer at Centerpointe Research Institute is called *The End® Personal Growth Through Technology*. We call it *The End* because we believe it is the last personal growth tool you'll ever need. *The End* is a curriculum of CDs or cassette tapes recorded with a powerful audio technology called Holosync®, which consists of precise audio tones directed into each ear and masked by soothing music and environmental sounds.

Holosync contains no spoken information or messages. Instead, using certain precise combinations of sine wave tones, Holosync creates in the listener the electrical brain wave patterns of deep meditation, causing the two sides of the brain to communicate in a new and beneficial way. As a result, Holosync stimulates a profound acceleration in mental, emotional, and even spiritual growth. Those who use Holosync experience the benefits of traditional meditation but receive these benefits much more quickly than through traditional meditation.

The program is easy to use. The daily practice consists of sitting comfortably, with eyes closed, either in a traditional meditation posture or in a comfortable chair, and listening to Holosync soundtracks through stereo headphones. At first, you listen for half an hour each day, and later, for an hour each day. Though this may seem to be a rigorous time commitment, participants look forward to their sessions—for a couple of reasons. First, the experience is almost always *very* pleasant, because the brain is stimulated to make several pleasurable and beneficial neurochemicals during listening. Second, as you will see, Holosync soundtracks are literally life changing, because they are *brain changing*, and this fact makes daily listening well worth the investment in time. And participants are always free to adjust their listening time to fit the demands of their lives.

As you listen, Holosync stimulates your brain to make structural changes that will increase your ability to

- Handle stress
- Meet challenges
- Tap into your creativity
- Accept people and situations with more equanimity
- Experience personal feelings of joy, inner peace, and happiness
- Understand yourself better

You may have listened to personal-growth audiotapes or CDs before, and had either positive or neutral experiences with them. I want you to know from the beginning that our program is different than anything you've tried before. I'll explain why, in some detail, in the following chapters.

Over the last decade, tens of thousands of people all over the world have enrolled in Centerpointe's program of self-exploration. I've drawn heavily on their experiences, their questions, and their insights in developing the program and in writing this book. I believe you'll find real value in reading about the adventures and experiences of others who have used the program as a vehicle for their inward journeys. You'll see how they've made their way through the often confusing and challenging journey of personal growth to a place where they know and experience themselves in a new way. And you'll read what they have to say about gaining inner peace and confidence in their role in the flow of life.

The Meditation Connection

As meditation became popular in the West, beginning in the late 1960s and early 1970s, advocates introduced many different approaches and, unfortunately, spread a lot of misinformation about meditation. At Centerpointe we talk to many people each day, some who have been meditating off and on for many years. While many have benefited from their meditation practice, others, regrettably, have very little to show for it. The mishmash of beliefs and misconceptions about meditation, what it is, how it works—and, particularly, how to know when you are doing it properly—is amazing. As a result, many are uncertain about whether they're meditating properly, what results to expect, and how quickly these results should appear. This uncertainty leads many to quit their practice with little or no result.

The idea behind meditation is really very simple. Doing it well, however, can be difficult, and mastering it may take many years. To meditate, you simply pay attention to a chosen point of focus—a mantra, a holy word, a prayer, the breath, or whatever—and whenever you realize you've been distracted (which can be often), you refocus.

Few scientists today dispute the benefits of meditation. Respected institutions, such as the Harvard University Medical School and the Menninger Clinic, offer programs of meditation for their patients. But many people, even with expert guidance, end up quitting, because meditation is hard to master, and results come slowly. Particularly in the first several years, the mind provides almost continuous distraction, and the meditator must continually focus and refocus the mind. This continuous need to refocus makes meditation difficult and often frustrating work, especially for Westerners who are used to instant results.

Meditation with Holosync keeps things very simple. You do not have to learn how to focus your mind as you meditate because the technology creates the same effect in the brain as focusing without your conscious effort. In fact, using Holosync actually creates a greater effect than does traditional meditation, leading to much faster results. Holosync meditation is also more precise and more consistent. It does away with the preliminary mastering of a technique

4

(which can take decades) and moves you directly to real changes in your life.

At Centerpointe, we know through years of experience and much study that you can reach success far more quickly using this program than through traditional meditation. This is not to denigrate traditional meditation, which I practiced for many years prior to my use of Holosync, and for which I have great respect. But the results speak for themselves, and results are what we're most interested in.

If you're experienced with traditional meditation techniques, you will find that the program allows you to meditate more deeply and create much greater positive change than you ever thought possible. And, if you've never attempted meditation because you didn't think you had the time or talent to devote to it, you will discover how easily you can fit this program into your life—and how quickly you can experience real, tangible benefits.

By participating in *The End,* you will be intentionally embarking on a program of personal growth. And, as is frequently the case with deep change, you may experience some upheaval from the process. This need not be bad or frightening; in fact, it indicates that old patterns of feeling, thinking, and acting are reorganizing into new ones that will serve you better. More on this later.

If a participant does experience upheaval as a result of the rapid positive changes taking place, we at Centerpointe support them every step of the way, in every way we can. We do so through a series of follow-up support letters, sent every two weeks during the first six months; through Centerpointe's *Mind Chatter* newsletter; through our web site; by e-mail; and through our always-available telephone hotline. Centerpointe also offers periodic retreats, at which attendees are able to experience Holosync in more depth and receive more personalized help with their personal growth issues. Our staff is familiar with the difficulties some people have as they work through the program and has years of experience answering the many questions people have. Believe me, we've heard it all! And, we have practical, proven answers.

An Overview of the Program

Over the course of the twentieth century, scientists discovered what happens in the human brain during meditation. They also discovered modern, technological methods of creating the brain wave patterns that characterize deep meditation, as well as other desirable states. At Centerpointe, we have incorporated the results of this scientific research into the audio technology we call Holosync.

How does this new technology work? Centerpointe soundtracks contain certain combinations of sine wave tones of precise frequencies embedded beneath soothing music and environmental sounds. When listened to through stereo headphones, these tones stimulate the brain to create the brain wave patterns of deep meditation. Because the tones are hidden, you don't hear them unless you really know what to listen for. What you do hear are beautiful and restful sounds, such as bells and falling rain. These sounds are merely cosmetic, however—it's the Holosync technology that really does the work. Two soundtracks are central to the program: a one half-hour soundtrack that gradually places you into deep meditation, and another half-hour soundtrack that holds you there. Each session is, therefore, an hour long. We recommend you do one session each day. There are additional soundtracks to enhance your experience, but this sequence is the heart of the program.

The entire program consists of an initial level, followed by twelve more custom-made levels. These custom-made levels are divided into three stages, each containing four levels, making thirteen levels in all. These levels are progressive, with each level creating deeper positive change. Each person begins with the initial program level, *Awakening Prologue*, regardless of their previous meditation experience. After you complete this first level, if you find yourself saying, "Wow! I really like what this is doing, and I want more," you can progress to the next level. Each level is complete in and of itself, and there is no pressure to go on to deeper levels—though most people do.

After *Awakening Prologue*, in addition to technological changes that make Holosync more powerful, we also begin to custom-make the soundtracks by adding silent affirmations chosen by you and recorded in your own voice. These custom levels are titled *Awakening Levels 1, 2, 3,* and *4*, followed by *Purification Levels 1, 2, 3,* and *4,* and finally by *Flowering Levels 1, 2, 3,* and *4.*

These levels take varying lengths of time to complete. The first level (*Awakening Prologue*) takes about four months to complete, although the exact time varies from person to person. The next three levels usually require about six months each, and the levels after that (*Awakening Level 4* through the end of the program) can take up to a year each to complete. As is explained in greater detail later in this book, in each subsequent level, Holosync stimulates your brain in such a way that the brain is pushed to reorganize itself at a higher, more functional, level. This reorganization creates some impressive positive changes in mental, emotional, and spiritual growth.

Although we provide guidelines to help you judge when it is time to move to the next, more powerful, level of the program, *you* make the final decision. As your brain adjusts to each level, you'll find that the "push" provided to the brain by the technology is not as powerful as it once was. Just like a runner who has run a mile each day until running a mile is easy, your brain will get to the point where it's no longer challenged by a particular program level. This happens because your brain has successfully created the new neural pathways and the new brain structures necessary to handle the Holosync stimulus used in that particular level. Once your brain has made these changes, it's time to move to a new and more powerful level of the program.

The Benefits

Almost immediately after beginning the program, people notice that their threshold for stress is higher. Difficult people and situations become easier to handle, without severe emotional reactions. Dysfunctional emotional problems, such as anger, fear, depression, anxiety, and substance abuse, begin to fall away. At the same time, thinking processes become clearer. An enthusiasm and zest for life emerges and grows. Often, one's purpose in life become more clear. These are the same results reported by those who spend decades practicing traditional methods of meditation—except that with Holosync, these results happen much faster.

Those who go deeply into the Centerpointe program also report another benefit—something a little more difficult to describe. In addition to inner peace, happiness, clarity of mind, self-awareness, and resistance to stress, participants also report an increasing experience of connection to the world around them, as well as a deeper connection to the Divine, God, Higher Power, the Universe (or however you understand the concept). And, people consistently report that this new way of experiencing life is immeasurably deeper and more rewarding than the stressed-out emotional roller coaster of a life they were living before the program.

Seeking this spiritual connection is not new, nor is it unique to users of Holosync. Most world religions advocate some form of meditation practice as a way of achieving mystical or experiential connection with the Divine. In addition, many people with no connection to an established faith seek a spiritual connection, through meditation, with the universe, life, or "what is." Seeking this connection is, in fact, one of the most universal of human aspirations.

Recent research suggests that there is a built-in human yearning for what scientists now call "unitary experience," and that this yearning has been a primary driving force in human evolution. This experience may even be the motivation behind many entirely secular and non-spiritual human activities.

According to research done at the University of Pennsylvania Medical School, the search for spiritual, or unitary, experiences is intimately interwoven with human biology, hard-wired into our brains. In their book, *Why God Won't Go Away*, researchers Andrew Newberg, M.D., and Eugene D'Aquili, M.D., Ph.D., describe the brain activity of meditating Buddhist monks and praying Franciscan nuns, at the exact moment of such unitary experiences. Using high-tech imaging techniques, Newberg and D'Aquili discovered that intensely focused spiritual contemplation (i.e., meditation or prayer) creates changes in brain activity, that lead to tangible yet ineffable experiences of oneness and connectedness with the rest of the universe. What Buddhists call "oneness with the universe," and Franciscan nuns call "being in the presence of God," are not the result of delusory or wishful thinking, but rather the result of a sequence of clear, discrete, observable, and recordable neurophysiological events.

Whether you think of yourself as religious or spiritual, or whether you completely reject such things, you are nonetheless hardwired to seek this unitary experience, and Holosync is a modern and effective—and relatively easy—method of achieving it. You can therefore approach this program from any religious point of view without compromising your faith. You can think of it merely as a way of reordering your brain to accept life's challenges and opportunities with greater equanimity and without fear. If you are part of a faith community, however, you can use your faith as the center for the work you do through Centerpointe. If you have no faith community, then think of it as a spiritual practice in any way you choose.

The Effects of Fear

One of the more common and sobering things we've heard from people using the Centerpointe program over the last twelve years is that many of them were raised in an environment of fear. Fear wasn't just something they felt every once in a while; it was pervasive—so pervasive, in fact, that most took it for granted, scarcely noticing it, like the fish not noticing the water. As adults, many of these people continue to live in a world of fear. Instead of dealing with it and resolving it in some way, they cope by distracting themselves with alcohol, drugs, sex, constant activity, and in a thousand other ways. For such people, coping becomes an undercurrent they're not aware of, but which affects everything they do.

As adults, these people often add new fears to those carried with them from childhood. They worry about relationships, about financial and personal success, about their children, about their futures, about their health, and about failing.

Despite the pervasiveness of these fears, and the real challenge in facing and resolving them, some people learn to move beyond them to live lives of well-being, happiness, and inner peace. These people can set goals and creatively move to successful, satisfying conclusions. They can form meaningful, loving relationships with the people around them, and can relate to challenges and adversity with equanimity and grace under fire. They can do these things because they've confronted and let go of fear-based perceptions and replaced them with confidence, self-awareness, and a feeling of connection to the world around them.

Confronting these fears isn't always easy. No one wants to

discover that the core elements of their worldview are rooted in false, fear-inspiring rules and proscriptions. But people who can confront their fears and move through them are then free to reach for their dreams.

One of the ways people grow through the Centerpointe program is by awakening to how much of their life has been structured around fear-based perceptions. As they move through the program, they replace this old way of seeing things with a new and more empowering view based on emotional balance, confidence, inner peace, and happiness. Although healing these old fears may be uncomfortable at times, facing them allows us to understand just how much of our sense of self-worth, success, and satisfaction had been hindered by these perceptions.

Interestingly, despite the fact that Centerpointe program participants have great insights into how and why they have created the events and results in their life, the changes people experience are generally *not* cognitive or intellectual. Rather, the changes manifest as the gradual dawning of a kind of internal "knowingness." Problems fall away, not because they are "solved" or understood, but rather because they become irrelevant. While intellectual understanding may come, it is a by-product of this much deeper spiritual understanding.

Not Knowing How You'll Get There

Many people believe that those who achieve what they want in life know, before they begin a project, not only *where* they are going, but exactly *how* they will get there—that they travel straight through to the conclusion by well-planned steps. This, however, is *rarely* the case. Ask any successful person if they went straight to their goal, and you'll probably get a chuckle followed by the long and winding story of what really happened.

It is true that successful people know where they're going, but very few start with a clear idea of how they'll get there. Napoleon Hill, author of the seminal work on success, *Think and Grow Rich*, has called this clarity and focus about the goal one's "Definite Major Purpose." Those who have worked through their fears realize that if they start toward their definite major purpose with whatever resources they have, the methods for achieving it will inevitably appear, as needed, as they move forward. In fact, taking the original steps toward the goal, no matter how tentative, is often the only way in which the plan for attaining it will appear.

Each of us comes to this process of growth and healing with his or her unique temperament, values, and background. Like all of us, you are a product of your early life and your own unique experiences with victory and defeat. If you're like most people, you have your own fears and barriers to growth. But if you make a start, and then keep going, no matter what twists, turns, and surprises confront you (and there will be some, I promise), this internal journey will truly allow you to heal past emotional traumas, feel contentment with your present life, and prepare you to face your future with power and acceptance. As you begin, don't let the fact that the path is unknown disconcert you or hold you back. Take the first step, and trust that what to do at each bend in the road will be revealed to you.

My Own Path

As I take stock of myself, I'm amazed at how content I am now, particularly considering where I started. Fear, anger, depression, and other dysfunctional feelings and behaviors used to be a constant part of my life, and the personal success I wanted seemed always to elude me. Before I began working with what later became Holosync, I spent most of my life *very* dissatisfied—with myself, with the world, and with other people. Everything was a strain, a crisis, a drama. Even my successes were unfulfilling because regardless of how good they were, they were never enough. I worried constantly. Because I was deathly afraid someone might find out I had needs, I was unwilling to open up and be vulnerable. I couldn't tell others what I wanted in a given situation because they might find out how *much* I wanted something, and this fear of being found out created an almost constant underlying anxiety. Because of the act I put on, most people thought I really didn't need anything, when inside I was really crying out for nurturing and love.

Why was I so afraid of opening to others? I don't know for sure. But because of it, I was often hostile and angry, and I succeeded in driving many good people from my life. Anger was the background of all my interactions, including those with myself. It was as though I walked around with a black cloud over my head. Because I was so unhappy, I was desperate to break that pattern, and went through many years of trying *anything and everything* that seemed like it might make a difference. I read hundreds of self help books, visited many different therapists, and attended countless personal-growth seminars. I learned to meditate, and practiced traditional medita-tion with great devotion and discipline for sixteen years. In my desperation I tried other more exotic approaches like firewalking, healing diets, and a number of other things I'm actually ashamed to admit I tried. A few of these things helped a little, for a while, but many, if not most, were a disappointing waste of time and money. Even when I thought I'd made progress, the old fear, anger, and depression would always return, which, of course, was very discouraging.

> ### PERSONAL EXPERIENCE
>
> "When I first started the Centerpointe program, about one year ago, I figured I'd pretty much come to terms with all my internal struggles and "ancient" history. Perhaps on some level I had, though some aspects of my internal life were still uncomfortable. The program definitely took me deeper, which is where I had to go to begin to flush out all the accumulated and "stuck" emotions, games, etc., that were still making my life miserable. At school, I was going through a particularly tough time, much of it beyond my ability to control. In the past, that would have absolutely enraged me. Now, I found that I was able to accept things as they happened and allow events to unfold without feeling that I had to affect the outcome of every situation. For the first time in my life I could step back, relax, and let go . . . and be okay with whatever the outcome was. The other students made comments about my newfound calm and peace of mind. I was promised in the literature, and I have to say that I definitely feel I am, functioning at a higher level now than I was before using the program."
> —Susan S., British Columbia, Canada

I know this sounds self-serving, but somehow the seven years of daily Holosync meditations I dutifully sat through finally trans-formed me. It allowed me to give up the old way I'd created—which believe me, wasn't working—and gave me the self awareness I needed to finally let go of the feelings, ways of thinking, and behav-iors that were holding me back.

I'm an ordinary person, but the combination of great persistence and determination to know myself, along with the luck I had in finding and using Holosync, have enabled me to take an inward journey that I hadn't thought was possible. Objectively speaking, it's the same world out there now as when I started seventeen years ago. But everything about me, about the world, and about other people seems different to me now.

I use myself as an example because I'm convinced that the kind of personal power and personal contentment I now experience is available to anyone, regardless of their past or present circumstances. You don't have to live in a world where you don't like yourself or other people, or where you use most of your energy each day just to hold yourself together. You don't have to live in a world where you're afraid to be close to other people, or where no one wants to be close to you. And you don't have to live in a world where others possess the power to live creatively and successfully, but not you. At this point, I've seen so many people create happy lives, regardless of their circumstances, that I know anyone can do it.

But what if you're already 100% emotionally healthy and living a life filled with fun, energizing projects, loving friends, and satisfying challenges? In that case, Holosync will make you even more effective, more internally peaceful, more clear in your thinking, and more self-aware.

If I've learned one thing from the last seventeen years, it's that the possibilities in life are much greater than most people imagine them to be, and that these possibilities really are available to anyone. After my own journey with Holosync, followed by over twelve years helping many tens of thousands of people use the Centerpointe program, I'm more firmly convinced of this than ever. Based on what I've seen, I can say without reservation that regardless of your current or past personal circumstances, *it is not necessary to live a life of suffering and unhappiness.* Happiness, inner peace, and personal fulfillment are available to anyone. If I can do it, you can, too.

Make Haste Slowly

Many people begin the Centerpointe program intensely dissatisfied with their lives. Many have read accounts of individuals who, despite the challenges they've faced, have learned how to live in great happiness and inner peace through meditation and other similar practices. Seeing these possibilities, and seeing the value of the Centerpointe approach, they often come to us in a mad rush to get from where they are now to where they want to be. They often dislike themselves, other people, and the world they live in. They are suffering, and they are in a hurry to end it. That's understandable. When I started, I was in a great hurry, too. There are, however, some pitfalls to hurrying this process.

I've said that Holosync technology allows you to get the benefits of meditation more quickly than traditional methods, but I want to be clear that I'm not saying that this is the "easy" way to grow and change. Though you don't have to spend years learning to meditate effectively, you *will* have to work through change.

Though people who have practiced traditional meditation for years often tell us, "Ahh, this is what I was told would happen when I first learned to meditate, but it never really did," the program still is not a "30-day miracle." From personal experience, I know that it took persistence and discipline over a long time to achieve the benefits I received. Others find the same thing. You cannot, for example, expect to meditate with Holosync for six hours a day and move through the program six times faster than we recommend. An

---

PERSONAL EXPERIENCE

"I've been meditating for almost 18 years now, and there have been huge changes in that time. But in the last two months, since I began the program, things are changing so fast it's hard to believe. Things I've been trying to get to the bottom of for ages, and really put in a lot of "work" on, are just dissolving beautifully. I seem to be seeing things so much more clearly, faster, and without the EFFORT. As far as I'm concerned the first level paid for itself in the first week and it just keeps getting better. I knew what my "problem" was intellectually, but I couldn't change it or get at it. So thank you for creating this great programme and I'm spreading the word."

—Judith B., New South Wales, Australia

hour a day is what we suggest, and for good reason: the brain is capable of benefiting only so much over a given time.

It's also not a good idea to race from one level to the next, thinking you're "more advanced" if you've somehow managed to quickly move to one of the stronger levels. A grade school student doesn't get much from sitting through a college chemistry class, and just being in one of the more advanced levels, without having fully integrated the changes from previous levels, is not going to make the changes happen any faster. In fact, it may slow things down.

Those who use the program as we advise, however, reap the rewards. I'm pleased by how often, a little more than half way through the program, people begin to say, "You know, I'm fine. Other people are fine. The world is fine. *Everything* is okay." A deep contentment begins to take over, and from that point on, the desperate urge to hurry is gone. From that point, people continue the program purely for the adventure of continuing to grow and improve, and to see what will happen next. Based on what's happened already, they know that whatever happens next, they're going to like it.

In explaining how the program works, I often use the analogy of a runner getting in shape because it's something everyone understands. Using Holosync is like running. You can run only a relatively short distance in the beginning of training. No matter how gung-ho you are, no matter how eager you are to be in great shape, you don't run a marathon the first week. Instead, you build up to it over a long time, increasing your running distance gradually, so that your lungs, circulatory system, and muscles can adapt to the stress. Eventually, when you've paid the price, your body is ready for serious running.

The Centerpointe program creates change at a very deep level, and does so more quickly than anything I've ever seen or used. Because everything will happen very quickly anyway, you don't need to hurry. So as you use the program, take your time, remembering the old Latin motto *festina lente*, "make haste slowly." You've undertaken a process of exploration, not a race. You may begin with certain goals in mind. You may think you know just what you need to change. But gradually, you'll be eager to proceed because you'll be making new discoveries about your capabilities and opportunities. You may achieve your original goals, certainly, or you may decide these goals weren't what you wanted or needed after all. But the real adventure is the discovery of new aspects of yourself and your environment that you didn't know could be so gratifying.

CHAPTER 2

⑥

When Meditation and Brain Wave Technology Meet

Even before I stumbled onto the advances offered by the new discoveries in sound technology, I was interested in meditation. I learned Transcendental Meditation in 1969, as did many college students in those days, and practiced it faithfully for many years. I later learned many other meditation techniques and approaches, some very advanced. I read many books exploring the subject of meditation from both ancient and modern scientific perspectives, and was fully absorbed in practicing the traditional approach.

I could see that people who meditated were more focused and serene, and I wanted these benefits for myself. The explanations for the power of meditation made sense to me. But reconciling traditional meditation (with all its beautifully metaphorical, but admittedly unscientific, explanations) with modern research into the structure and operation of the human brain was the real breakthrough for me. In creating this link between science and meditation,

I felt I'd found a powerful, new tool for self-understanding and self-transformation.

There May Be Two Sides, But It's Still the Same Coin

To understand why Holosync® technology accelerates the rate at which one can receive the results available from traditional meditation techniques, let's start with a bit of philosophy. Mystical explanations of the origin of the universe state that the one energy of reality (the same unifying energy physicists have now identified from a more scientific perspective) polarized itself at the moment of creation into apparent dualities—good and evil, male and female, up and down, here and there, and all other pairs of seeming opposites. I say "apparent dualities," and "seeming opposites," because in each pair of opposites each part is dependent on the other for its existence, like two sides of a coin. "Cold" is meaningless except in relation to "hot"; "good" makes no sense without "bad." According to the mystical philosophies of the East, it is the tension in our mind between these pairs of opposites that causes the universe to manifest.

Interestingly enough, this tension between opposites is also reflected in the structure of the human brain. The brain, divided into right and left hemispheres, mirrors the dual structure thought

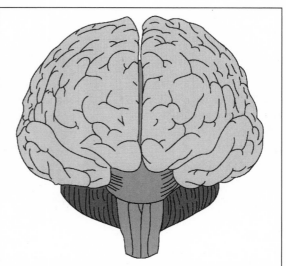

The dual structure of the brain. For most functions, the right side of the brain controls the left side of the body, while the left side of the brain controls the right side of the body. The dual structure of the brain, in combination with hemispheric dominance, affects the way we see the world.

by mystics to be a central characteristic of the universe. This innate duality of the brain is made more acute by the fact that in virtually all people, the two hemispheres are unbalanced, a state called *brain lateralization*. Because the brain filters and interprets reality in a split-brained way, we tend to see things as separate and opposed, rather than as connected and part of the oneness spoken of by the great spiritual teachers (and, in the last few decades, by quantum mechanical physicists).

Thus, at a deep level, the dual structure of our brain, in conjunction with *brain lateralization,* predisposes us to see and experience ourselves as separate from, and often in opposition to, the rest of the world—instead of experiencing the elegant interconnectedness between us and everything else. Our childhood associations and programming build on this inborn tendency by training us to seek this and avoid that, to move toward pleasure and away from pain, to do good and not bad, and so on.

The greater the lateralization in the brain, the greater the feelings of separation—and the greater the feelings of separation, the greater the fear, stress, anxiety, and isolation. In its extreme form, a lateralized, unbalanced brain results in behavior commonly described as "dysfunctional" or "addictive," with all the painful feelings that accompany those states.

In traditional meditation, the meditator seeks to eliminate the effects of brain lateralization through some form of focusing, such as repeating a prayer or mantra, keeping the attention on the flow of the

In 1975, Herbert Benson, M.D., an Associate Professor of Medicine at the Harvard Medical School and Chief of the Division of Behavioral Medicine at Beth Israel Deaconess Medical Center, published *The Relaxation Response.* This book describes studies at Harvard Medical School in which subjects experienced the same states, and received the same benefits, as practitioners of traditional meditation, just by sitting with eyes closed and repeating a single word, such as "One," silently to themselves for twenty minutes a day. These benefits included dramatic reductions in stress, lowering of high blood pressure, relief of chronic pain and insomnia, and mitigation of a multitude of other complaints.

One of Benson's most important contributions was demonstrating that a focus on anything creates a meditative state in the brain, with all the attendant benefits.

18

breath, staring at a candle flame, or one of several other techniques. Whatever the technique, the effect on the brain is substantially the same: synchronization of the two brain hemispheres—and after much practice, an experience of connection with the rest of the universe, accompanied by profound inner peace and happiness. Any kind of focusing will bring about a degree of brain synchronization. The greater the focus, the greater the synchronization, and the deeper the meditative state.

As the meditator focuses, he or she moves from what scientists call a *beta* brain wave state, typical of normal waking consciousness, into a slower and more relaxed *alpha* brain wave state. Later, after many years of disciplined practice, the meditator gains enough mastery to begin brief excursions into the deeper (and even more relaxed) *theta* brain wave state (more on these brain wave states in a moment).

> **PERSONAL EXPERIENCE**
>
> After being on *The End* program for almost two years and attending two retreats, I am convinced that Centerpointe has developed the most effective transformational program on the market today. I make this claim based not only on my own experiences, but also on the experiences of my spouse, my father, and one of my friends. They are also on the program. For me to say that I have witnessed remarkable changes in myself and my loved ones would be the understatement of the millennium! Words cannot even begin to describe the depth of change that I have witnessed in myself and others.
>
> —José I. Rodriguez, Ph.D., *Mind Chatter* No. 40

As the meditator accesses these more relaxed meditative brain wave states, there is an increase in communication (and therefore balance) between the two sides of the brain, and a reduction in feelings of stress and separation. At first, this more balanced and less stressed state is temporary, lingering for only a short time after meditation. But changes in the brain over time, including the creation of new neural connections between the two brain hemispheres, gradually lead to an ability to enter these states at will, even when not meditating, and remain in them for longer and longer periods. One way to look at this might be to say that as the brain balances, the meditator's threshold for what he can handle coming at him from his environment gradually moves higher and higher, making him increasingly immune to stress-related problems and ailments.

Unfortunately, as I have said, this process is slow. It can take years, even decades, to perfect the ability to reach and stay in these slower brain wave states, and still longer for the changes they cause to really take hold.

Because Holosync creates these same brain wave patterns—precisely, consistently, and without effort—it allows the Holosync meditator to skip the long and tedious process of perfecting meditation skills and get right to the business of creating positive change. The process is further accelerated because Holosync actually creates even deeper meditative states than are possible through traditional techniques. Interestingly enough, Holosync meditators find their ability to meditate in a traditional way also dramatically increases as they become regular users of the Centerpointe program.

Meditation alters the filter through which the outside world is perceived. The more balanced synchronized brain is less likely to split reality into categories based on arbitrary, early-life programming. Dualities become less divisive, the unity and interrelationship of all things becomes more apparent, and one begins to experience life as a connected whole. People engaged in serious meditation are more able to live without fear and judgment, without the need to manipulate others, without automatic

---

Information You Can Use— Our Brains are Us

"Neuroscience is coming of age. We are beginning to understand a lot about the brain, and several things follow from that. We will be able to have a better life. Our brain is us. We will be able to keep our brains in better shape. The quality of our life depends very strictly on the quality of brain function that we have. We will be able to increase the quality of brain function with age, so it doesn't deteriorate, so we remember properly and we function properly and we can then really enjoy being old.

"I go to the dentist once a year to see how my teeth are doing, but I don't think of going to the neurologist to see how my brain is doing. Clearly our brain is more important than our teeth. We can have false teeth; false brains are not around."

—Dr. Rudolfo Linas, Chief of Physiology and Neuroscience at the New York University School of Medicine

negative responses to life's ups and downs, and without a desperate need for approval—in short, without the limitations of mental programming, especially that based on separation.

Extensive research has demonstrated that this balancing, or synchronization, of the hemispheres of the brain happens in all forms of meditation. The degree of hemispheric synchronization can be very precisely determined by measuring the meditator's brain wave patterns with an electroencephalograph (EEG).

Brain Wave Patterns and Their Meaning

In 1970, Elmer Green, Ph.D., of the Menninger Foundation, studied Swami Rama, an Indian yogi who lived in the United States. Under laboratory conditions, under the observation of research scientists, Swami Rama demonstrated many ways in which internal states thought to be outside conscious control could be regulated voluntarily. These studies gave researchers the first peek at the brain wave patterns of meditation. The studies are described in *Beyond Biofeedback* by Dr. Green and his colleague, Alyce Green (New York: Delacort, 1977). Shortly thereafter, research scientists associated with the Transcendental Meditation movement of Maharishi Mahesh Yogi also conducted extensive studies that allowed researchers to observe the brain wave patterns of the meditative state.

Over time, additional research demonstrated that the brain generates different wave patterns, progressively longer and slower, as meditation becomes deeper. Scientists have identified the following brain wave patterns, named with Greek letters:

> • *Beta pattern. This is the fastest pattern: 13–100+ Hertz (Hz, cycles/sec). This is the common pattern of normal waking consciousness and is associated with alertness, arousal, and concentration. Except for unusual circumstances, we create some combination of all four categories of brain waves at all times. For most people, most of the time, however, beta waves are of greater amplitude, or strength, than the others, and are therefore the most prominent. We now also understand that higher-end beta waves (30 Hz and higher) occur during times of uneasiness, distress, and anxiety. Dysfunctional and addictive behaviors, neurosis, and strong*

21

feelings of separation are common experiences when the brain operates in the extreme high end of the beta range. The extremes of the beta range are also associated with what scientists call the "fight or flight response."

• **Alpha pattern.** *This pattern is somewhat slower: 8–12.9 Hz, and occurs soon after closing your eyes and relaxing. Alpha brain waves are associated with introspection. In the alpha state, the body produces calming neuro-chemicals. At the higher end of its range it produces what has been termed a "super learning" state. When you are deeply absorbed in a book, for instance, you are probably making an increased amount of alpha waves. Pre-sleep or pre-waking drowsiness occurs at the lower of the alpha range. Deep alpha (i.e., the lower end of the alpha range) is also associated with peace and contentment, and is the predominant brain wave pattern of traditional meditation. While beta is part of fight or flight, alpha (and slower) waves create what Dr. Herbert Benson of the Harvard Medical School termed the relaxation response. In this state, instead of being mobilized to deal with external danger, we are turned inward for introspection, learning, relaxation, and renewal.*

• **Theta pattern:** *This pattern is slower still, between 4–7.9 Hz. This is the pattern of rapid eye movement (REM) dreaming sleep, sometimes called a hypnagogic state. Theta is associated with enhanced creativity, memory, healing, and integrative experiences, where we put together previously disparate pieces of information, leading to an "ah-ha" experience or sudden understanding. Generally, even very advanced meditators attain the theta state for only moments at a time. Studies of Zen monks have shown momentary bursts of heightened theta during meditation. Many psychologists believe the theta state is the doorway to the unconscious mind.*

• **Delta pattern:** *This is the slowest pattern, between 0.1–3.9 Hz. It is the pattern of dreamless sleep. Some have postulated that in delta we make contact with what Swiss psychiatrist Carl G. Jung called the "collective unconscious" shared by all humans. A great feeling of unity and oneness is experienced in delta. At the same time, it is possible to be alert in this state, as long as there is a small amount of beta, alpha, or theta patterns. While some delta waves are happening all the time*

in the brain of every person, meditators do not enter a pre-
dominantly delta state (unless they fall asleep, in which case
they are no longer meditating). However, using Holosync you
can enter a predominantly delta state and remain there for
long periods of time.

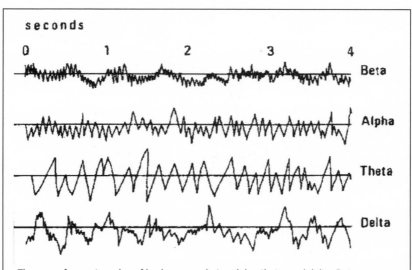

There are four categories of brain waves: beta, alpha, theta, and delta. Beta waves
are of the highest frequency. In their highest extreme beta is associated with anxiety,
unease, and lack of inner peace. At the slower end of the beta range, focus and
cognitive thinking increase. Slower than beta are alpha waves, associated with focus,
"superlearning," and meditation. Still slower are theta waves, associated with
dreaming sleep, increased creativity, some kinds of learning, and extremely deep
meditation. Deepest of all are delta waves, associated with dreamless sleep and
many autonomic nervous system functions. Notice that the height of the wave form,
also called the amplitude, increases as the frequency slows. Amplitude corresponds
to power, one reason why slowing the brain waves using Holosync provides a more
powerful "push" to the brain.

In each Holosync listening session the soundtrack gradually
takes you from the higher levels of alpha, down through alpha, then
through theta, and finally into delta. However, we specifically focus
on the delta pattern because we have found that this is where the
greatest acceleration of growth takes place. This ability to hold you in
the delta state—something you cannot do through traditional
meditation—is another reason why Holosync causes such profound
acceleration in your growth.

When we enter the alpha and theta brain wave states during
sleep, we scan data stored in the unconscious parts of our mind and,

to a certain extent, re-arrange and process it. This scanning and processing we call dreaming. As we move into the alpha and theta states, we become more aware of the unconscious parts of the mind. This means that non-resourceful mental programming (old, inappropriate feelings and behaviors that usually run on automatic and do not give you the results you want) is accessible in theta, allowing it to change to something more resourceful (more on this later). Finally, in the delta state, we access areas of the mind where the broadest and most primal programs about what it means to be human are stored. Meditators using Holosync soundtracks are able to remain alert and

---

PERSONAL EXPERIENCE

I have been listening to Holosync for almost a year now and I am feeling so great it's almost unbelievable. I feel like a different person. Stress that used to bother me isn't as bad now, and I am actually happier or more content. My back is doing better and isn't going into spasms when I am confronted with conflict. I am more relaxed and happy to talk about problems rather than being afraid. And if I do get upset, it lasts only a few minutes, rather than days, and it isn't as overwhelming. Every day used to be a struggle for me. I had no desires and even wondered "what am I living for?" Now, I'm accepting what is and dealing with the problems positively and working on solutions. I still have bad days but it's so much better than it used to be, and now I know I'm getting stronger and healthier, younger everyday. I'm so happy to get rid of dysfunctional feelings and be able to be happy around people instead of uncomfortable. This is a dream come true for me.

Thanks, Ruby S., *Mind Chatter* No. 85

---

aware in the delta state, even though delta is a sleep state. From what these people have told us about their experiences, we know that delta allows a meditator to access material from the deepest levels of the unconscious. Amazingly, our experience at Centerpointe has been that merely accessing this mental programming while in a meditative state seems to change it in a positive way. What is more, the Holosync meditator doesn't even need to consciously know what is being changed or have any intellectual knowledge of what is going on. The intellectual understanding of what has changed comes *after* the change has occurred, and doesn't even seem to be necessary!

Inducing Brainwave States Through Technology
☉

At about the same time research on the connection between brain waves and meditation was moving forward, Dr. Gerald Oster, of Mt. Sinai Medical Center in New York, published a paper in *Scientific American* (October 1973) about research he had been conducting since the 1950s into the effects of sound waves on brain wave patterns. Oster's paper described a method, using very precise sound waves, that allowed a person to create any desired electrical pattern in the brain, including the patterns of meditation.

Dr. Oster found that certain waves occur in the brain as it reconciles sounds of slightly different frequencies to create one rhythm. The sounds enter as separate inputs, one in each ear. After being received as separate tones, a part of the brain called the olivary nucleus generates a single consistent wave pattern that is a resolution, or reconciliation, of these tones.

After the publication of this research, a small industry sprang up around this technology and its ability to alter brain wave patterns. These early efforts focused on stimulating the brain to generate particular brain wave patterns that were thought to bring about desirable experiences. Experimenters would say, "We'll put you in an alpha brain wave pattern, and you'll experience increased learning ability," or, "We will put you in a theta state, and you'll become more creative." To these early experimenters, the goal was to enter these states in order to have certain pleasurable experiences, or to experience an increase in certain mental abilities associated with those states. As we'll see, I came to believe that, while this certainly does happen, there was something much more profound going on— something everyone else was missing.

How Centerpointe Began
☉

Back in 1985, I began experimenting with what eventually developed into the Holosync audio technology we now use in the Centerpointe program. Up to that point, I had done my meditation straight and unaided, the old fashioned way. But one day, a friend gave me a cassette tape and told me it contained a sound technology that would put me in a deep meditative state. I was polite, but told him I thought the idea was ridiculous: "People have been meditating in a certain way for centuries for a reason. If there was a better way, some great meditation teacher would have already thought of it." I was reluctant to even try it.

About three weeks later I happened to wear the same jacket I'd been wearing that day and found my friend's cassette in the pocket. "What's this?" I thought. "Oh, yes. The high-tech meditation scam." But I stuck it in my Walkman, put on some headphones, and tried it.

Some twenty years ago British biofeedback researcher C. Maxwell Cade began working with an EEG [electroencephalograph] specifically designed to show full-spectrum brain-wave activity. As he worked with hundreds of people who were able to function exceptionally well, who were able to enter heightened states of consciousness easily, he began noticing similarities in the patterns of brain waves they produced.
As he compared these exceptional people with his thousands of other subjects, he noticed that there was a distinct progression. In the first stage, most people could soon learn to enter the alpha state, in which beta diminished and alpha became the dominant frequency. As they progressed in their practice, many of these people learned to enter the theta state, in which beta, alpha, and delta diminished and theta became dominant. In this, his findings matched those of the EEG studies of Zen monks.

But Cade found that exceptional people, those who were peak performers, soon moved into a different pattern. When they were in their peak state, their EEG patterns showed that their brains were producing large amounts of alpha and theta as well as strong beta and delta activity—all at the same time.

Cade called this extraordinary brain-wave pattern the Awakened Mind. He found that these peak-performance individuals could maintain this pattern even while reading, performing mathematical calculations, and carrying on conversations! Apparently these individuals were able to draw upon the relaxing, centering properties of the alpha state, the creative, memory-accessing properties of the theta state, the healing, "grounded" properties of the delta state, and at the same time still maintain the alert concentration and external orientation of the beta state
—Michael Hutchison, Mega Brain Power, 33–34

The images on the following pages are brain wave patterns of subjects connected by electrodes placed on their scalp to a Mind Mirror, a type of EEG machine. The bars on the left represent activity in the left brain, and those on the right represent activity in the right brain. The length of the bar as it expands out from the center respreseents the amplitude, or relative strength, of each brain wave pattern. Moving from top to bottom in each diagram, each bar represents a different frequency, with the top five bars on either side representing beta waves at 38, 30, 24, 19, and 15 Hz, respectively; the next three bars representing alpha waves at 12.5, 10.5, and 9 Hz; the next three bars representing theta waves at 7.5, 6, and 4.5 Hz; and the bottom three bars representing delta waves at 2.75, 1.5, and 0.75 Hz.

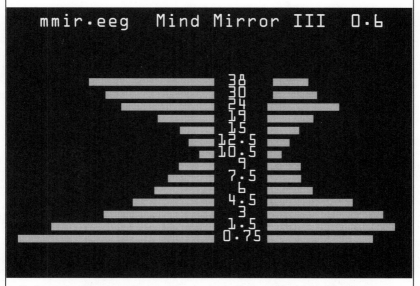

mmir.eeg   Mind Mirror III   0.6

Brain waves of a non-meditator with eyes open. Notice the lack of balance between the left and right hemispheres, with higher amplitude in the left hemisphere showing concentration or controlled attention. Also notice the very low amplitude of alpha waves. The higher amplitude in the delta area is the result of unconscious, autonomic nervous system functions.

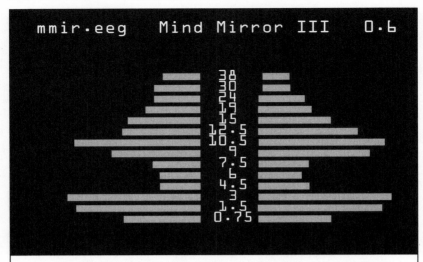

Holosync meditator listening to Holosync designed to induce alpha waves. Notice the low amplitude of beta waves and high amplitude of alpha waves, indicating deep relaxation. The relatively high amplitude of delta waves is associated with unconscious autonomic processes.

Holosync meditator (eyes closed) listening to a soundtrack designed to enhance delta brain waves in the 2.5 Hz range. Notice the high amplitude of the bars representing the delta range, the smaller amplitude in the other brain wave patterns, and a slightly greater amount of alpha (the result of the other sounds on the CD). Note also the relative balance between the two sides of the brain.

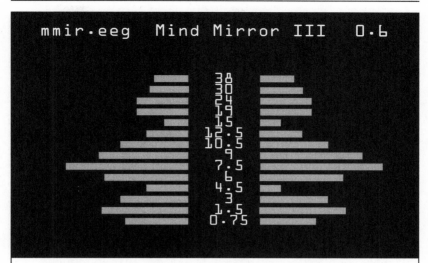

Long time Holosync meditator with eyes closed (not listening to Holosync). Note the relative balance between the brain waves in each hemisphere, the peaks in amplitude in each of the alpha, theta, and delta areas, and the relatively small amplitude in the beta area. This pattern is very similar to that of the "Awakened Mind" identified by researcher Maxwell Cade.

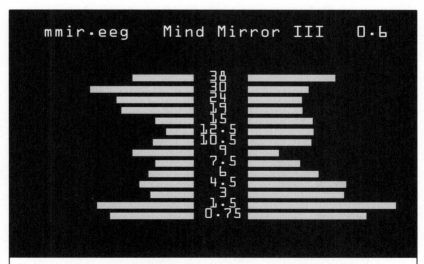

Experienced Holosync meditator in resting state eyes open (not listening to Holosync). Notice the relative balance of all four brain wave types, and the relative balance between left and right hemispheres, which corresponds to whole brain functioning. The relatively high amplitude of all brain wave patterns, without any areas of extremely low amplitude in any frequency, indicates that tor this person the conscious and unconscious areas of the mind can share information.

Information You Can Use—
Do You Want To Know The Details?

I make available to anyone who wants it a survey of scientific research relating to what we do, complete with footnotes and bibliography. In addition, I make public a selection of excerpts from letters we've received from people in the program, plus a list of prominent doctors and other experts who have endorsed the program, and a list of other prominent people in the personal growth field who have also endorsed the program.

All of this is posted on our web site, www.centerpointe.com. A discussion of this research can be found at the back of this book, in Appendix I.

It was 10 minutes long, but it really impressed me. I had an incredible meditation, better than a really "good" day after 45 minutes or so of traditional meditation. Though it was tough for me to reconcile my reaction with my conservative orientation, I had to admit there was obviously something to it.

I began doing some research and reading about the effects of sound on the brain. Eventually, I borrowed some tone generators and other equipment from the University of Portland engineering lab, where I was a graduate student in music, and started making my own soundtracks for meditation. A group of us started using these soundtracks, and over the next four and a half years we became convinced, based on the extraordinary progress we were making, that something really remarkable was happening.

Those four and a half years changed my spiritual awareness, my emotional health, my personality, and my life. My friends and I noticed, within a fairly short time, that we were having many of the classical meditation experiences we'd read about in various scriptures and accounts of famous yogis and other meditators. Despite being disciplined, long-time meditators, we'd never (or rarely) experienced these levels of deep meditation, even after years of practice.

These experiences, however, while often intriguing, are not really the point of meditation—traditional or technological. What I found much more significant was that we began to notice real improvements in mental ability, inner peace, happiness, and self-awareness. As these positive changes continued to happen, we knew we really had something. In late 1989, with one of the people who had been experimenting with me, I started Centerpointe Research Institute.

30

The Centerpointe Breakthrough

Some time after our initial euphoria, the initial pizazz of our meditation experiences began to level off. We'd reached a plateau where not nearly as much was happening. We were disappointed, to say the least. "So much has happened," we said, "and we've had so many amazing changes. It's a shame we're not being pushed to grow anymore." What a letdown it was after we thought we'd found THE answer. But, rather than let it drop, I was determined to find out *why* this plateau had occurred. I began to examine the prevailing idea that the most important thing was to place yourself in a particular brainwave pattern. Something told me there was more to it than that.

I finally concluded that everyone had missed the obvious: *it wasn't being in the pattern that counted most; it was that being in certain brain wave patterns forced the brain to do more work, pushing it past its current threshold for what it could handle.* Others were concentrating on superficial effects and were missing the deeper and more significant underlying processes actually responsible for the changes.

The level of technology we'd been using, (now called *Awakening Prologue*), pushed our brains past their former mental and emotional thresholds, just as a one-mile run might push a beginning runner past his physical threshold. But after a while, our brains had finished creating the new structure they needed in order to handle the Holosync stimulus. Once that happened, they were no longer being pushed, which was why it seemed as if we'd reached a plateau. At this crucial point, I asked a question that no one else in this field was

Centerpointe Insight—Relax and Enjoy The Ride

We try to counsel people to not spend too much energy trying to minutely evaluate the day-to-day changes or what experiences did or didn't happen, but rather, to just put in their listening time each day and look back at their progress periodically. This allows you to relax and enjoy the ride. Take it as it comes and just watch with curiosity whatever happens. Although it is not always easy to do, I've found this to be good advice whether you're talking about *The End*® program or life in general.

asking: "Is there something else we can do, something we haven't noticed yet, to increase the amount of input we're giving the brain so that we'll be able to continue the evolutionary changes we've been enjoying so far?"

Although no one in the neurotechnology community was framing it in these terms, I began to think of the brain as reorganizing itself at higher, more complex levels of functioning in response to a stimulus that was beyond its ability to handle—rather than just reaching a certain brain wave pattern and then, as a result, exhibiting certain states or increased mental abilities. How, I asked myself, could we increase the power of this stimulus, and therefore increase the "push" the brain was receiving? We were already putting ourselves into a delta state, where the electrical fluctuations were the most powerful. What else could we do? In answer to the question, I began to look at something called *carrier frequency*.

Centerpointe Insight—The Goal is Resiliency

Some systems look at brain waves and attempt to make up deficiencies. I don't believe the goal is to get into certain brain wave patterns, although that is an effect of listening to Holosync. Our goal is to create plasticity, resiliency, and flexibility in the brain so a person can enter whatever state, or combination of states, that is appropriate to what is happening around them or to what they want to accomplish.

Carrier Frequency

To understand carrier frequency, you have to understand a simplified explanation of how we induce the different brain wave patterns with Holosync. First, we introduce a tone of a certain frequency into one ear, and a tone of a slightly different frequency into the other ear. The brain must reconcile the slight difference in frequency between the two tones. To do this, a part of the brain called the *olivary nucleus* creates what is called a *beat pattern* in the brain, corresponding in frequency to the *difference* between the two tones. This *difference tone* acts like a tuning fork, causing the brain wave patterns to resonate in sympathy with it, a phenomenon scientists call *entrainment*.

The carrier frequencies, then, are the frequencies of the pair of tones used to generate the third tone. If we make the difference between the two tones 10 Hz, for example, the predominant brain wave pattern will become 10 Hz, in the middle of the alpha range (8–12.9 Hz).

As long as the difference between the two tones is 10 Hz, your brain will resonate to a 10 Hz alpha state. Notice, however, that there are an infinite number of pairs of tones that could be used to induce a ten-cycle-per-second alpha state. If, for example, we began with carrier frequencies at 230 Hz and 240 Hz, we would be inducing a 10 Hz alpha brainwave (240 minus 230 equals 10). If we then lowered the two frequencies to 190 Hz and 180 Hz respectively, we would still be generating the same 10 Hz alpha state (190 minus 180 equals 10) *but using a lower carrier frequency.*

> ### Information You Can Use— Sounds of Meditation
>
> There are two reasons why we have musical crystal bowls and rain as a background for our soundtracks. One is just to mask the Holosync tones and give you something pleasant to listen to. The other is to give your brain something to hold on to, to help you produce some high-end alpha and beta brain wave patterns, so you maintain some alertness and are less likely to drift away while you're in a delta brain wave pattern.

I became intrigued with the possibility that lowering the two tones we used—in other words, the carrier frequencies—might provide the extra push to the brain we were looking for. And, when we tried it, that's exactly what happened: as we lowered the carrier frequencies, Holosync became much more powerful, and the evolutionary changes that had so disappointingly leveled off began again, even more powerfully.

Once we determined that lowering the carrier frequencies would indeed create a more powerful effect, we naturally wanted to find out just how low we could go. So, being young and reckless (well, reckless anyway), we created some ultra-low-frequency soundtracks and started listening to them every day. At first we became extremely

---

PERSONAL EXPERIENCE

I don't actually meditate. My thoughts seem to flow endlessly. Sometimes I just let it be, and other times I feel like controlling them and do it, concentrating on something specific (like my breathing). Sometimes I fall asleep. Sometimes I feel an urge for the CD to end and other times I just don't want them to, wishing I could remain in that state foreeeeever.

—Chara G., *Mind Chatter* No. 29

---

euphoric as the brain flooded us with endorphins and other pleasurable neurochemicals, but within four or five days we were freaking out—mentally, emotionally, and even physically. We had so much mental, emotional, and even physical "stuff" coming to the surface that we were totally overwhelmed by it. This was an object lesson. Just as a runner increases his running distance gradually over time, we had to move to lower carrier frequencies gradually, allowing the brain to adapt before moving to the next level.

From this extremely uncomfortable and rather frightening experience, we developed the idea of having an on-going program in which we would start people with a carrier frequency that would be challenging to the nervous system, but not overwhelming. We wanted to push the brain to change, but not so fast that people couldn't handle it.

Then, after several months of daily use, when the nervous system had finally come to the point where it had made all the neurophysiological changes it needed to make in order to handle the input it was receiving—when the soundtracks didn't seem to feel very strong anymore—we moved to something stronger by lowering the carrier frequencies. Each time we did this, a new and even deeper set of changes, different for each individual, would began to happen.

Lowering the carrier frequencies allowed us to continue to stimulate growth and to get much more from this type of technology than others in this field were getting. This discovery changed the technology from an interesting curiosity, or a way to experience interesting altered state experiences, to something very substantial that had the ability to create powerful core-level changes in mental, emotional, and spiritual health.

It Takes Both the Beat Frequency and the Carrier Frequency

ⓖ

There are two ways, then, that Holosync gives the nervous system input, or stimulus, that pushes it to reorganize at higher levels of functioning. One is by slowing the brain from a beta brain wave pattern to an alpha pattern, then to theta, and finally to delta. The second is by lowering the carrier frequencies used to induce these alpha, theta, and delta brain wave patterns.

We use both, something that distinguishes what we do from others using sound technology to change brain wave function. Holosync technology uses precise and specific tones to take the listener into the brain wave patterns of meditation. It creates fluctuations in the brain that push it to create a new and more complex structure, and it causes the brain to create new neural pathways linking the left and right brain hemispheres in order to process the slightly different signals given to each side of the brain.

But we also need the increasingly lower carrier frequencies. Otherwise, we would end our journey after a few months. Once the brain finished creating the pathways needed to handle the first set of frequencies we originally gave it, evolution would stop. We would be like a runner who could never increase his run to two, three, or more miles.

In terms of the running analogy I've used, lowering the carrier frequency is like adding more miles to your run. The lower the carrier frequency, the longer the run. On the other hand, the meditative brainwave pattern caused by the *beat frequency* the brain creates

Q & A—Does music ever do what Holosync does?

The frequencies of the tones we use are quite close together, less than a half tone apart. It's unlikely that the effects achieved through our sound tracks would ever be induced through music, and certainly not in any predictable way. Music can relax you and maybe it can put you in a light alpha state. But music's ability to create a sustained state below that is virtually nonexistent. We use very sophisticated audio equipment to create sine wave tones calibrated to an accuracy of 3/1000 of a cycle per second.

Q & A—If I stop using Holosync, do the benefits go away?

As the originator of the program, I finished the Centerpointe program in 1992. I now meditate with Holosync only a few hours *each year,* but the benefits still continue for me. Using the program creates a momentum in your growth that continues long after you stop listening. The neural pathways created by the program are used all the time as you think, feel, respond to your environment, and go about your life—unlike running muscles, for instance, that need continued training to maintain the same amount of conditioning. Even though I completed my work with Holosync over ten years ago, I continue to have a threshold for what I can handle that is so high that almost nothing can move me off-center. In fact, it's higher than it was when I last regularly listened to the program soundtracks.

in reconciling the two Holosync tones corresponds to how *fast* you run. Slowing the brain waves from beta to alpha to theta to delta is like running increasingly faster. By allowing us to run faster *and* farther, carrier frequency allowed us to really push the brain to change.

Keeping the Brain Supple
☺

Carrier frequency was the master key that really allowed us to take full advantage of the Holosync technology and to continue the process of change far beyond the point where other neurotechnology approaches became ineffective. This is why—even though completing just one level of the program creates tremendous change—it is so important to continue into the deeper levels. By gradually increasing the input to the brain through increasingly lower carrier frequencies, the benefits increase exponentially, and people continue to experience positive growth for many years.

It's difficult to quantify and describe the depth of change possible through stimulating the brain with Holosync. Even people who come to the program convinced they've worked through all their mental and emotional issues are continually surprised to find deeper and deeper levels of positive change as they go deeper into the program.

As more profound levels of awareness and inner resources unfold for them, they feel transformed in ways they couldn't have imagined when they started. I have to admit, if I hadn't experienced it myself, and observed it in tens of thousands of people, I wouldn't have believed it myself.

CHAPTER 3

☙

Open Systems and the Human Mind

Often a moment of crisis, no matter how small, is exactly the
point at which we begin to see things in a new way. Something is lost, but new possibilities appear. As we begin to
move through such a period of intensity, we're more open to change,
especially if the crisis forces us to see that what we've been doing, or
how we've been seeing things, no longer works. Through the crisis
and because of it, we can accept information we might have been
ignoring, avoiding, or simply not seeing. We're surprised to find that
we can now deal with situations, people, or events that once seemed
impossible. The crisis doesn't have to be a national or global event; it
can be quite personal and internal. It turns out that crisis can be—
and often is—a positive change agent.

But emergencies aren't the only facilitators of change. We don't
have to face dramatic or threatening circumstances in order to
experience personal evolution. The human brain is a complex, self-
regulating system, able to integrate experiences of amazing complexity. In response to changes in the environment, our brains construct

new pathways and reconstruct old ones. In other words, the human brain has the quality of *plasticity* or *malleability* throughout life—*if* it receives the kind of stimulation that allows it to grow and adapt. We can think of the brain, the nervous system, and the conscious mind as partners able to capitalize on changes in the environment.

During the last 100 years scientists in both physics and biology have learned a great deal about how complex systems such as the brain evolve when placed under appropriate stress. Think of how athletes get stronger as they place their bodies under the stress of exercise, and you'll grasp the essence of the idea. Holosync® soundtracks stress the brain in a precise and very beneficial way, one that causes the brain (and you) to grow and become stronger. This type of growth and change helps you meet and accept the world in a new way: calmly, with confidence, and without fear.

In this chapter I discuss the theory of systems evolution on which our program is based. I want you to understand the mechanism of how positive mental and emotional changes happen, how the Centerpointe program facilitates these changes, and why—for years—our clients have experienced the results they have.

Entropy, Chaos, and Quantum Leaps

This may, at first, appear to be a detour to an arcane topic seemingly unrelated to personal growth. Bear with me, however. The following information lays the groundwork for a most elegant description of how personal growth and positive change happen, while at the same time giving us some valuable clues as to how to accelerate the process and make it much easier.

During the industrial revolution of the nineteenth century, science was exploding with new discoveries. Many of these discoveries occurred as a result of common observation. One of them, a basic law of thermodynamics, was discovered when physicists began to measure the energy lost—that is, energy that could not be accounted for—in the process of converting fuel into work.

Physicists thought that, ideally, a perfectly efficient heat engine could perform a work cycle that would convert all the available heat into mechanical work. According to the second law of thermodynamics, however, this is impossible. Nicolas Carnot (1753–1823),

Q &A—
Shouldn't meditation be internally silent? What do I do about all the mind chatter I experience?

It is not true that to meditate properly your mind must be still. The end result of years of meditation is a still mind, but the process itself is often one of upheaval, with lots of thoughts and lots of distractions.

In traditional meditation, you must focus on something (such as a mantra, the breath, or a prayer) in order to create the brain wave patterns of meditation. Focusing slows the brain wave patterns into meditative states. Thoughts or other distractions will, however, continually pull you off focus. This happens because the mind's purpose is to create thoughts and notice things. As soon as you notice your thoughts have drifted to something other than your point of focus, you gently pull your mind back. You may be distracted two seconds later, at which point you once again go back to your point of focus as soon as you notice you've been distracted. This process happens over and over in a typical meditation. Some days it happens more, on others, less. Everyone experiences this during the first several years of traditional meditation.

This process of focusing, losing focus, re-focusing, losing focus again, re-focusing again, over and over, can be tedious and frustrating. This, and the fact that results come very slowly with traditional meditation, often over decades, is a major reason why many people give up in frustration.

With Holosync you don't need to focus because the technology, not your focusing, creates the brain wave patterns of meditation. Thus, there's no need to keep pulling your mind back to a point of focus, though many people like to do a focusing technique while they listen because they've been meditating for years and it's a habit. Doing this, however, isn't necessary. With Holosync, you can just watch your mind do whatever it wants to do. While you still have to deal with the mental, emotional, and spiritual changes created by your meditation, Holosync make the *technique* of meditation easy.

who conceived the thermodynamic cycle that is the basis of all heat engines, showed that such an ideal engine cannot exist in the real world. Any heat engine must expend some fraction of its heat input as exhaust, heat radiation, friction, and so forth.

Thus, the second law of thermodynamics places an upper limit on the efficiency of engines, and that upper limit *has* to be less than 100 percent. The implication of this law of physics is that *over time all things tend to break down and become less ordered, unless energy is added in some way*. Another way to understand this is to say that whenever work is done, some energy is irretrievably lost. The measurement of the inefficiency of the process is called *entropy*. Entropy can also be thought of as a measure of the *disorder* or *chaos* in a system or as the measure of the amount of *randomness* in a system.

In fact, the same law predicting the creation of entropy in the energy exchange that powers machines applies to all energy systems. The law of entropy applies to cosmic entities like stars and planets, to systems within a single planet (such as weather), and also to chemical, electrome-chanical, biological, and social systems.

It is a basic law of nature that the net amount of entropy in the universe is *always* increasing, and this law of increasing entropy is an expression of the fact that

Information You Can Use— How Entropy Works

In converting coal into the energy used to power a steam-driven piston, not all the energy in the coal is turned into motion. A certain amount of energy is lost. When the coal is converted to steam power and the expanding steam causes a piston to move, some energy is lost from the system due to friction dissipated in the form of heat radiation. In addition, the machine itself (unless energy is added to the system in the form of an overhaul, new parts, etc.) will eventually wear out and break down. The movement of a piston within a cylinder will eventually cause the piston to break down. In fact, all machines, all systems, all things, will break down unless more energy is added. A car will turn to rust and fall apart, a mountain will eventually be worn down, the club you belong to will disband, and so on. Even the expansion of the universe itself is a movement in the direction of increasing disorder, increasing entropy.

the universe is irreversibly moving toward a state of increased disorder and randomness—it's running down. Left to itself, with no energy input from the outside, the universe, like all other systems, irrevocably moves toward increased disorder.

Yet we can plainly see that many things in the universe tend toward *increased* order—the opposite of what is predicted by the second law of thermodynamics. The history of living organisms on earth shows life becoming more ordered and *less* random. Life has evolved as atoms formed molecules, molecules combined into amino acids and proteins, proteins formed single cells, single cells combined to form multicellular living organisms, and multicellular organisms eventually evolved into *Homo sapiens*, with his elaborate social systems. This process leads from less order to increased order and increased complexity. It seems to be completely at odds with the accepted principle that the amount of entropy in the universe is irrevocably increasing. How is it possible, scientists wondered, that some things can evolve and grow and become more ordered when the overall tendency in the universe is for things to break down and become less ordered?

It took over one hundred years for scientists to find an answer to this intriguing question. The answer came in 1977, in the Nobel Prize-winning work of the Russian-born, Belgian theoretical chemist, Ilya Prigogine. Prigogine became intensely curious about this major contradiction between one of the basic laws of science and equally basic observable facts, including the existence and evolution of life.

Open Systems

⑥

Until Prigogine's time, physics had focused its study on idealized, *closed* systems; that is, systems with no interaction with the surrounding environment. This reduced the number of variables to a manageable number. Researcher found that closed systems soon reached an equilibrium state of maximum disorder. For example, you probably remember from chemistry class that molecules of hydrogen in a closed container spread out randomly, and any chance ordering that occurs is immediately offset by an offsetting tendency toward increasing disorder. The net effect is to maintain an equilibrium state of maximum entropy.

Prigogine, on the other hand, wanted to solve the riddle of why and how systems of increasing order and complexity can exist in a universe inevitably tending toward disorder and chaos. To do this, he studied *open* systems—highly complex systems that interacted with their environment. Studying certain chemical processes—open systems that, when heated, exhibited increased order and growth— his results again seemed to contradict the second law of thermodynamics. Subsequently, through mathematical analysis of his results, he solved the riddle: he learned that while open systems did indeed become increasingly ordered, *they did so by dispersing entropy to their environment.*

Prigogine proved his hypothesis that order emerges not *in spite* of chaos but *because* of it, that evolution and growth are the inevitable product of open systems slipping into temporary chaos and then reorganizing at higher levels of complexity—and higher levels of functioning. Such systems take in energy and matter from the environment, but more important, they dissipate the resulting entropy from the system and into the environment. Thus, the overall

Up Close

Ilya Prigogine, (1917–) is a Russian-born Belgian physical chemist and Nobel laureate. For his pioneering work in non-equilibrium thermodynamics, The Nobel Committee awarded Prigogine the prize for chemistry in 1977.

Born in Moscow, Prigogine left Russia with his family in 1921 and settled in Brussels, Belgium. He studied chemistry at the Université Libre de Bruxelles, receiving his doctoral degree in 1941 and becoming a professor there in 1947. While maintaining his ties in Brussels, in the 1960s Prigogine joined University of Texas at Austin as professor of physics and chemical engineering. He subsequently founded the Ilya Prigogine Center for Studies in Statistical Mechanics and Complex Systems, at that university.

Prigogine's theories are used in the study of biological systems and have even provided models for theories in fields such as economics, meteorology, and population dynamics. His eloquent book *Order Out of Chaos* (1983) helps explain his research to nonscientists, a task he felt was an important part of a scientist's work. He has also published *From Being to Becoming—Time and Complexity in the Physical Science* (1980) and *Exploring Complexity* (1989) (*Microsoft® Encarta® Encyclopedia 99.* © 1993–1998 Microsoft Corporation).

energy result *does* follow the second law of thermodynamics: overall, entropy increases, but not within the system itself.

Prigogine called open systems that operate in this manner *dissipative structures*. Other scientists have since confirmed that Prigogine's discoveries regarding dissipative structures apply to every open system in the universe, whether a chemical system (as in Prigogine's original experiments), a germinating seed, a highway system, a corporation, a social system, a star, or an individual human being.

Dissipative structures, in order to maintain their existence, must interact with their environment, by continually maintaining the flow of energy into and out of the system. And rather than being the

Closed System	Open System
At equilibrium	Far from equilibrium
Rigid, non-resilient	Plastic, adaptible, resilient
Little or no exchange or interaction with environment	Does interact with environment, constant exchange of energy and matter with environment
Static, stable, do not evolve	Dynamic, a flow, ability to grow and evolve
If stimulated, outcome of change predictable using Newtonian physics	If stimulated, outcome of change unpredictable (can be predicted only with probability theory)
Cannot dissipate any build-up in entropy; excess input leads to death of the system	Ability to dissipate entropy to the environment in order to maintain structure
	Have upper limit of how much entropy they can dissipate; the more complex the system, the greater its ability to dissipate entropy and the greater its resiliency

structure through which energy and matter flow, *dissipative structures are, in fact, the flow itself.* This supports a view, reached independently by physicists studying quantum mechanics, that the universe is not a universe of independent, separate entities, but rather one of process: a changing, flowing, evolving, and intimately interconnected system of interactions.

Open systems maintain (or even increase) their orderliness instead of breaking down because they have the ability to get rid of entropy. But here is a key point: although open systems are extremely plastic and can handle all kinds of fluctuation and variation in input from their environment, each system has an upper limit of how much randomness—how much entropy—it can dissipate to its environment. This limit is based on the system's structure and its degree of complexity: *the greater the complexity of the system, the greater the amount of entropy it can dissipate.*

Because each system is really an on-going flow of energy, the limit of how much entropy can be dissipated also puts a limit on how much *input* the system can handle. This limit is the system's *threshold.* As long as the input level does not exceed the ability to dissipate the resulting entropy—in other words, as long as the input does not exceed the system's threshold—everything is fine and the system remains stable. But once this limit is exceeded, the system will be unable to dissipate some of the entropy. As a result, chaos begins to build, and order breaks down.

Information You Can Use—Highway Evolution

A highway system is an example of an open system. It is relatively stable, and can handle relatively large fluctuations in traffic and traffic patterns. If, however, the amount of traffic suddenly increases to a point where there isn't enough room for all the cars, the system becomes chaotic. But eventually the input lessens, as rush hour (or other cause) ends, and cars cease to overload the system. But if the system develops chronic chaos, highway engineers will widen the road and add more lanes and on/off ramps, sometimes completely reordering the landscape. The new highway construction allows the system to dissipate the entropy (chaos) the old system could not. This new system is more complex, and more stable—unless congestion increases to a point where once again there is too much input.

How Open Systems Evolve

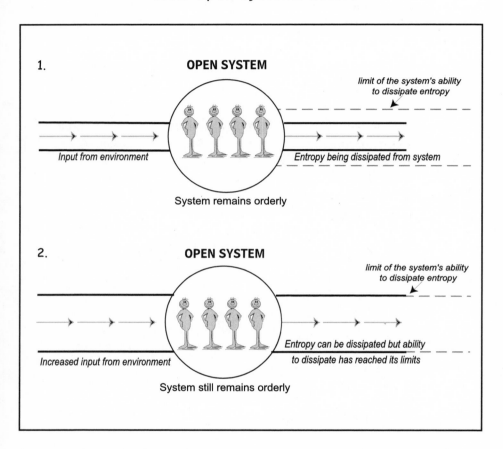

Each open system has an upper limit of how much entropy it can dissipate (dashed lines). As long as input from the environment does not exceed this threshold, the system remains orderly. This is because dissipation of entropy to the environment prevents its build-up inside the system. In the first figure, the amount of entropy being dissipated is below the system's threshold, while in the second figure, the amount of entropy being dissipated has reached the threshold level. In either case, the system is able to dissipate all entropy and maintain its structure and orderliness.

In the third figure (next page), input from the environment begins to exceed the system's ability to dissipate the resulting entropy, which begins to build up in the system. As a result, the system begins to become chaotic. As this continues (fourth figure), the system finally reaches a point of maximum disorder, leading to a momentary breakdown of the system and two possible outcomes: either the system breaks down and ceases to exist as a viable system, or it evolves to a higher, more resilient, and more functional level that can dissipate the entropy the old system could not (i.e., the threshold for how much input can be tolerated increases).

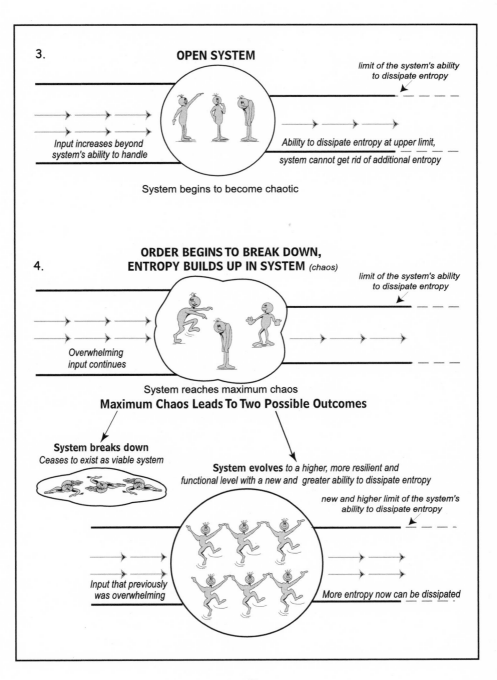

3. **OPEN SYSTEM**

limit of the system's ability to dissipate entropy

Input increases beyond system's ability to handle

Ability to dissipate entropy at upper limit, system cannot get rid of additional entropy

System begins to become chaotic

4. **ORDER BEGINS TO BREAK DOWN, ENTROPY BUILDS UP IN SYSTEM** *(chaos)*

limit of the system's ability to dissipate entropy

Overwhelming input continues

System reaches maximum chaos

Maximum Chaos Leads To Two Possible Outcomes

System breaks down
Ceases to exist as viable system

System evolves *to a higher, more resilient and functional level with a new and greater ability to dissipate entropy*

new and higher limit of the system's ability to dissipate entropy

Input that previously was overwhelming

More entropy now can be dissipated

If the input continues to exceed the system's ability to dissipate the necessary entropy, the system will continue to become more chaotic and more unstable. Open systems are very plastic in their ability to handle fluctuations in the amount of input they receive, but if input continues at a level exceeding the threshold for long enough, the system will eventually become so unstable that the slightest nudge can push it over the edge. This point, which Prigogine called a *bifurcation point*—bifurcate means "to divide into two branches"—is a moment of truth.

At the bifurcation point, either the system totally breaks down and ceases to exist as an organized system, or it spontaneously reorganizes itself *in an entirely new way*. An open system, as it reorganizes, has, literally, an infinite number of potential outcomes. Think of an angry crowd on the verge of rioting, or a hive of bees ready to swarm. Because the number of variables is so large, only the *probability* of any specific outcome can be determined, not the certainty.

Evolutionary Growth—Escape into a Higher Order

ⓖ

The most significant thing about this reorganizing process is that the new system is, in fact, totally non-causal and non-linear with what went before; rather than a variation on the old, it is something totally new. The old system has ceased to exist and a new system has been born. In Prigogine's words, the system "escapes into a higher order." It is a true quantum leap, a true death and re-birth. One of the most important characteristics of the new system is that *it has the capability to handle input from the environment that caused the old system to become overwhelmed and break down*. If the stimulus or stress increases again to a level beyond the new system's new and higher threshold, the process will repeat. A new buildup of entropy, if it continues for long enough, will lead to another reorganization at a yet more evolved, more complex, and higher level.

Living things are clearly open systems. Far from achieving equilibrium, they constantly take in energy in such forms as light, heat, nutrients, air, water, and sensory stimuli. At the same time, they dissipate to their environment carbon dioxide, heat, and waste products, as well as dissipating entropy through the performance of various activities. In this way they are constantly in flux, constantly

Something to Think About—All Things Are Connected

In light of Prigogine's work and the study of dissipative systems, we begin to understand just how connected *all* systems are. There are many examples. But it's obvious that the output of one system as it dissipates energy to its environment is the input to one or many other systems. In this way it is easy to see how an event in one system—located within a human being or in one part of the globe—can affect virtually all others in some way, to a greater or lesser extent.

Because we know that all systems are connected, we focus not so much on the systems as separate entities, but on the connections between them, since that's where the exchange occurs. We begin to look at the flow rather than at the discrete objects within the flow.

If we observe the suffering of others and decide not to take action because we think it doesn't affect us personally, we're denying our ultimate connectedness to the world. If we choose to see suffering only in terms of something that negatively affects us directly, we fail to realize the deeper truth: that our evolution—as individuals and that of humanity in general—depends upon our ability to see beyond the confines of ourselves as separate entities.

adjusting to their environment, constantly changing, growing, healing, and learning.

This process of chaos and reorganization is the mechanism by which evolution happens. All things grow and evolve in this manner. In fact, this process repeats itself millions of times each minute in every cell of your body. As each cell gets to the point where, as a single cell, it is unable to dissipate the necessary entropy to maintain its structure, it either dies or reorganizes at a higher level by dividing into two cells. Eventually, aging or disease diminishes the body's ability to efficiently dissipate entropy to the environment, and death is the result. Remember that physically, emotionally, and mentally we are complex systems that obey all the laws discussed above, just as do all other complex systems in the universe. And, beyond the biological, our cognitive and psychological lives are also complex open systems.

Both personal growth and personal suffering become much more understandable when we consider them in terms of this model. For example, core beliefs and personal ways of dealing with what happens in your life change and evolve as old ways of looking at and

---

Centerpointe Insight—Peak Experiences

It's easy to see that certain types of people will be more likely to reach what psychological researcher and theoretician Abraham Maslow (1908–1970), one of the founders of humanistic psychology, called "peak experience"—and give themselves the chance of "escaping into a higher order." Those who constantly open themselves to new ideas and experiences and who are not afraid of feeling a bit overwhelmed once in a while are more likely to have this type of peak experience. They are, therefore, more likely to evolve, to experience their model of reality reorganizing at a higher level of functioning. On the other hand, people who habitually resist new ideas, who resist new experiences, who reject what does not fit the structure of their belief system and have trouble acknowledging doubts about their ways of seeing things—in other words, people who resist the influx of new energy, stimuli, and ideas—rarely have peak experiences because they are blocking their potential to evolve. Those with this outlook evolve very slowly, if at all.

---

dealing with the world are overwhelmed by ever-changing input from your environment. There comes a time when old attitudes and habits just don't work any more, and must change. Think of the beliefs and issues that were important to you at age eight. As you grew older and your environment changed, your beliefs, personal issues, and the way you saw both yourself and the world changed and evolved in response to this new input. As you grew older your model of the world grew increasingly more complex and you learned to deal with increasing amounts of input.

So now, perhaps, you see where I'm headed. I want to present human beings as open systems and as flows of energy. We are more than our brains and our bodies, we are the flow of energy through them; we are the evolving, organic process of life itself.

The Human Mind, an Open System

As we have seen, the process of reorganization is continuous at the cellular level as long as there is life. Some cells are reorganizing at a higher level, and some are dying. We are unaware of these microprocesses, but with powerful microscopes and other imaging machines, we can document the process. We don't yet completely understand, however, the intricate workings of the conscious and unconscious minds. We don't know, for example, how to track the evolution of an individual's perception of reality, or the way in which a person's worldview changes over time.

But we can think more clearly about such matters by understanding the human mind as an open system that functions in the same way as other open systems. The mind is constantly exchanging energy with its environment. This energy is in the form of both physical and emotional input. If the input or stimulation increases to a certain critical point (different for each individual), we begin to feel stressed, and eventually overwhelmed. As a result, we become less and less able to deal with what is happening. We have reached a *threshold*. Our old assumptions are challenged and our habitual ways of dealing with life are no longer effective. They may, in fact, no longer make any sense to us, when only a moment before they seemed to be the most normal and sensible mechanisms and outlook we could imagine. When we reach a threshold, things become chaotic, and we feel uncomfortable, even overwhelmed. If this chaos continues long enough, our whole way of seeing things may break down. Metaphorically at least, we fall apart. And then, just as in Prigogine's model, our mental construct of "what is" reorganizes itself at a higher, more evolved level. Once this happens, things make sense, but in a whole new way, one that we could not have imagined before.

Applying the Model to the Human Mind
ⓖ

Understanding this systems-model of change and how it applies to the development of personal growth in human beings leads to an obvious question. What would happen if a set of stimuli were to be purposefully designed to give the human brain input that would cause our current way of being and operating in the world—our model of who we are and how we respond to the world—to go through this highly beneficial evolutionary sequence of *overwhelm*, *temporary chaos*, and *reorganization at a higher level*? We wouldn't be doing this to cause a "breakdown" in a conscious, debilitating sense,

These three photographs show water droplets magnified on a slide and "excited" by sound vibrations. In response to the vibration, mandala-like ordered shapes are created. The top picture shows a five-sided pattern. In the picture on the lower left, the power of the vibrational stimulus has been increased to a level beyond the ability of the five-sided system to handle, which causes the five-sided figure to become chaotic and begin to break down. After a few moments in this chaotic interim state, the droplet suddenly takes on a new and more complex structure, a ten-sided shape shown in the picture on the lower right. Though these "excited" water droplets are not true open systems, they do demonstrate visually the Prigoginian process of order, increased input, chaos, and reorganization at a higher level.

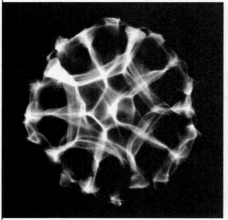

Images from *Cymatics: A Study of Wave Phenomena and Vibration*, © 2001 MACROmedia, Used by Permission. MACROmedia, 219 Grant Road, Newmarket NH 03857. www.cymaticsource.com

but rather to increase our personal resiliency and to allow us to deal more clearly, more calmly, and more resourcefully with whatever happens. What if, in doing so, we were able to create a totally new way of being, one that's more internally peaceful and happy and outwardly more effective? If the stimuli or fluctuations affecting the brain were strong enough, and applied in just the right way, even a brain strongly resistant to change could be caused to evolve to higher levels of mental, emotional—even spiritual—functioning.

PERSONAL EXPERIENCE

There was a time when I found nothing magical, nothing mysterious enough, to give anything of myself except my fear. Fear determined much of my outlook on life for a while, but slowly the fear melted away and was replaced with a sense of awe and wonder, and perhaps even a deeper sense of peace beneath it all. But even this sense of peace was not constant until recently. That is not to say that I began to feel my old fears, but rather that I began to "settle in" to a sense of comfort that was not fueled by my own experiences, but rather by the memories of the experiences that brought me peace in the first place. I am now having the same experiences that I had in the first place again. That is, noticing the "coincidence" in my life that brings me to a new place, spiritually. Noticing seemingly insignificant things in my life and realizing that they are there for a reason, they are there for me to discover and learn from. In fact, finding Centerpointe was one of these coincidences. I "asked" for a teacher who could help me meditate. I just asked, nobody in particular; I was by myself. And the next day I "happened" to bump into The Daily Guru on AOL, where I found out about Centerpointe. My teacher would turn out to be Holosync.

—Dan, *Mind Chatter, No. 54*

This is exactly the purpose of Holosync audio technology. Holosync gives the brain more input than it can handle in the way it is currently structured, and this leads the brain to reorganize itself, over and over, at higher levels of functioning. This is the process: increasing stimulation to the brain ⇒ temporary overwhelm of the current system ⇒ reorganization at a new and higher level ⇒ increased capacity in the person for awareness, emotional health, mental abilities, and the understanding of life experiences in a greater context.

In studies at the University of California at Berkeley in the 1970s, researchers placed laboratory mice in enriched environments containing mirrors, swings, ladders, little tunnels to run through, and so on. Later, when the researchers studied the brains of these highly stimulated mice, they found them to be much larger and more complex, and containing many mores types of cells associated with intelligence, than the brains of mice that had not been stimulated in the same way. In a similar way, Holosync audio technology creates a super-enriched environment for your brain, encouraging new connections, complexity, and resiliency that otherwise would not develop.

When you use Holosync soundtracks each day, you subject your brain to stimuli that push it to the point where it must, in Prigogine's words, "escape into a higher order." Then, as you move to successively deeper levels of the program, you create the same alpha, theta, and delta brain wave patterns, but at carrier frequencies increasingly lower in tone and larger in amplitude. This carefully orchestrated increase in brain stimulation results in changes in the deep structures of the brain. You can tell these changes are occurring because you see yourself easily handling more and more complex stimuli in your daily life.

> ### PERSONAL EXPERIENCE
>
> When I first started *The End* program about one year ago, I figured I had pretty much come to terms with all my internal struggles and "ancient" history. Perhaps on some level I had, though some aspects of my internal life were still uncomfortable. *The End* definitely took me deeper, which is where I had to go to begin to flush out all the accumulated and "stuck" emotions, games, etc. that were still making my life miserable.
>
> —Susan S., *Mind Chatter No. 3*

One of the exciting things about moving from one level of the Centerpointe program to the next is that there is no way to predict the specific experiences any one person will have, or exactly how the process of change will unfold. Initially, some people find this unsettling; they prefer to have the future mapped out for them, so they can prepare for what tomorrow holds. But, in a process that mirrors the way life actually happens, Holosync users enter a world of discovery, surprise, and serendipity.

Although I've already said this, it's worth repeating that the course of evolution is not always easy. Personal evolution takes time and work. And some of the work includes passing through mental thresholds, points where stimulus exceeds capacity. Be assured that Holosync technology is *designed* to cause your brain to arrive at and pass through a series of thresholds. But as you arrive at these thresholds, you may experience some temporary disturbance until you complete the process of reorganization. Threshold disturbance is neither permanent nor dangerous. It isn't even necessarily uncomfortable, as you will see. But it is a normal part of the process. In Chapter 4, I'll discuss what thresholds are and how you can recognize them. Then, in Chapters 5 and 6, I'll discuss how to move through thresholds with the least difficulty and the most success to the positive growth on the other side.

ALL OF WHAT WE KNOW IS PHYSICALLY EMBODIED IN OUR BRAINS. TO INCORPORATE
THE NEW KNOWLEDGE REQUIRES A PHYSICAL CHANGE IN THE SYNAPSES OF OUR
BRAINS, A PHYSICAL RESHAPING OF OUR NERVOUS SYSTEM.

—GEORGE LAKOFF

CHAPTER 4

The Process of Change

One of the great things about having many thousands of
people in the Centerpointe program is that we've become a
living laboratory, learning how people grow and change.
There is constant two-way communication between our staff and
Centerpointe program participants about the rewards—and challenges—of the inner journey. Through our newsletters, Web site,
telephone support, retreats, and personal e-mail correspondence,
we're delighted to offer support, encouragement, and tailored advice.
In turn, our clients let us know when they want our help and input,
and they share with us their personal stories.

In this chapter, I want to talk about the process of change, a
process important to all human beings. At Centerpointe, we know
that inner growth has two aspects, conscious and unconscious.
Conscious change happens within our awareness and in the com-
pany of our intentional direction and guidance. More common,
however, is unconscious change, in which changes happen outside
our awareness. Most of the change that happens to Centerpointe
program participants happens on the unconscious level, though
conscious awareness of what's happening can speed up the process.

I realize that discussing conscious and unconscious as two different aspects of the same process artificially separates them. In reality, change happens as a result of the subtle and complex interplay between conscious and unconscious factors. But it's helpful to know the specifics about both parts of the journey. Therefore, I offer a model that encompasses both conscious and unconscious change. A simple way to understand how conscious and unconscious intersect as you use the Centerpointe program is to think of the whole process this way: listening to Holosync soundtracks brings to the surface unconscious material that you can use consciously to help yourself change and grow.

The Six Stages of Conscious Change

Over the years many Centerpointe program participants have shared with us their experiences in making intentional, conscious changes—the kind of changes that occur when you're aware that something interesting is going on inside your psyche, you're anxious to allow it to emerge, and want to aid the process. As a result of this feedback, we developed a six-step change model that describes in a general way how participants first encounter changes, then examine them, and finally incorporate them into their understanding of who they really are and how they want to operate. I want to thank transpersonal psychologist Dr. Beverlee Marks Taub, Ph.D., for her help in formulating this model of the change process:

1. *Awareness.* In this first step you begin to realize that some part of your map of reality is being stirred up as it begins the process of changing to something more functional and more resourceful. As previously unconscious parts of your internal map come into conscious awareness, you may experience discomfort, unrest, confusion, or other symptoms. This awareness is the beginning of the end of your ability to continue acting from patterns of thought or behavior that don't serve you. The discomfort results from the fact that you associate the old way of being with safety and at some level are afraid to let it go (more on this in a later chapter). As you are pushed to your threshold for what you can handle, the possibility of raising that threshold opens. Even

though your awareness of these unconscious patterns may still be intermittent, and you may still want to deny they exist, you have reached a point where you're getting ready to do things differently.

2. **Identification.** In this second step, the physical sensation, feeling, thought, or emotion becomes strong enough that it becomes difficult to suppress, repress, or deny it. At this point you can identify more specifically what is happening ("I'm feeling angry," or "I feel resistant to this"). It is important at this point not to get stuck in denial. It is a very healthy sign to be able to say, "This upheaval is part of the change process. It's not something that's happening to me from outside of myself, but rather a response coming from within me." This honesty with oneself prepares you to take the next step.

3. **Focusing.** In this step the energy of the feeling, thought or emotion is heightened and fully felt. This is a crucial point in the process. It involves total ownership and responsibility: "This is my anger. I'm not a victim of some outside force. I'm having this feeling, this response, due to my particular internal mental programming." This is where you let whatever is happening be okay, rather than resisting the fact that it's happening. Instead of resisting what is happening, you watch with curiosity. Unlike the first two stages, in Stage 3 you must focus your conscious intention in order to overcome the tendency to become unconscious again through distractions, such as food, television, drugs and alcohol, sex, mental analysis, and so on.

4. **Expansion.** In this step you become aware of the core belief system that lies behind your behavior and your reactions. Because you've been watching what is happening with curiosity, your awareness expands and you are able to generalize about past experiences and possible future situations, seeing patterns in how you have been creating suffering for yourself around this issue. Be aware that your mind will create whatever is necessary to prove the "truth" of its programming, and core beliefs will manifest as reality in your life. To determine what your core beliefs really are, then, it is necessary only to look at what is happening in your life. If you are creating unhappy relationships,

for example, the core belief may be some version of, "No one will ever love me," "I am unlovable," or "I have to give up my autonomy in order to be loved." Another clue in uncovering core beliefs is your internal self-talk when in the depths of despair: "No matter what I do, it's never good enough," "There's something wrong with me," "No one will ever love me."

This is a crucial step in the growth process. It once again involves taking responsibility for what is being created. Responsibility in this context does not imply blame, but rather than your unconscious programming (which you probably didn't choose) is responsible for your experience, not external forces (although outside events can act as triggers). In other words, when we take responsibility we can't be victims. When we are not distracted or diverted by denial or the idea that we are a victim of some outside force, and we choose not to distract ourselves by dysfunctional behaviors, we can honestly look at what is happening and see the core belief that lies behind it. Doing so continues the process of bringing into conscious awareness what has been unconscious.

5. **Resolution.** In this step you fully experience the feeling, thought, or emotion at its peak, but this time in a completely conscious way. This constitutes a major shift in awareness. It signifies that your old way of seeing yourself has reached a point of chaos, and can now reorganize itself at a higher level. This change, the replacing of an old, outmoded way of being with one that is more resourceful for you, happens because of a fundamental fact about personal growth: it is not possible to continue doing something that is not good for you, and also do it with full awareness. Non-resourceful feelings, behaviors, and ways of being can only be continued as long as they are automatic, unconscious responses. Once you bring full awareness to the feeling or behavior, if it is not resourceful for you—if it creates suffering—it will fall away and be replaced by something that does work for you.

6. **Reintegration and Reprogramming.** In this final step, you incorporate the new way of seeing things into your internal map of reality. That which was previously a source of pain now becomes a strength. You no longer see it as something to be

repressed and avoided, and it no longer exists as an automatic response unconsciously creating suffering for you. It is replaced by behaviors and feelings that are more conscious, intentional, and resourceful.

Following these steps is not always easy, even if you fully understand them. It takes real practice to consciously recognize your

Six Stages of Conscious Change	
1. Awareness	• Discomfort, unrest, confusion; may experience uncomfortable emotions; old way of seeing or responding, cannot maintain inner balance; change becomes possible
2. Indentification	• Thought or sensation too strong to ignore or deny • Becomes possible to indentify what is happening ("I'm angry.") Realization and acceptance that what is happening is coming from within is important
3. Focusing	• Important to stay conscious rather than distracting oneself with dysfunctional coping mechanisms • Feeling, thought, or emotion fully felt • Total ownership and responsibility of what is happening • Very helpful to acknowledge that whatever is happening is coming from within
4. Expansion	• Become aware of core belief that lies behind your behavior and reaction • Awareness expands to include realization of patterns in past and present behavior; ability to generalize to possible future consequences
5. Resolution	• New generalization is made that is more resourceful
6. Reintegration and Reprogramming	• Full experience of feeling, thought, or emotion but now in a completely conscious way • New behavior becomes fully integrated

feelings, accept responsibility for them, and to own them. It takes practice to stand back and watch what is happening and to realize in real time that no matter what is happening to you, you can choose your response to it. It takes time to accomplish the shift from unconscious reactor to conscious responder. In Chapter 6, I'll discuss in more detail a way of witnessing your own process so you can become a curious observer rather than a psychic sufferer.

Ironically, though unconscious, automatic responses create suffering, we often tenaciously hang onto them. Why? Because while growing up we create a model of who we are and how we relate to the rest of the world, and we do so in a way that creates the greatest feeling of safety for us in our family situation. When we go out into the world as adults, this model of who to be and how to behave often doesn't work as well as it did in our family. In fact, it often creates problems. So, we seek change; however, if we find something that really works to create change, often a part of us unconsciously says "What? Change? Are you kidding? This way of being has kept me safe all these years."

Centerpointe Insight — The Importance of Conscious Intention

Resolution, more than any other step, requires conscious intention and heightened awareness. At this stage of the process, you must simply be a witness to what is going on. This means instead of resisting the recently uncovered non-resourceful programming, you must watch its continued manifestation with full awareness, as if you were an intensely curious scientist, not wanting to miss a single detail of how this particular bit of programming manifests as life experience.

It's important to note that you do not accomplish this "witnessing" by trying to stop doing things in the old way—you do it by just watching whatever is happening with undivided awareness and curiosity. This awareness causes you to see the unvarnished truth concerning all the pain this particular core belief has caused you. Before this point, you've remained unconscious enough to blame things on someone or something else, or to distract yourself from really feeling the pain involved. The brain immediately seeks a new way of being that avoids this pain; that is, it evolves. As long as we see the cause as being outside of us or we distract ourselves in some other way, the brain will hang onto the old way of seeing things.

And so, we unconsciously resist the very change we want and need, and this resistance creates discomfort and suffering.

Thresholds
⑥

To help you better understand the six steps above and the process people go through as they experience major psychological change, let's look more closely at the concept of *threshold* that I introduced earlier. You'll remember that the moment when a personal threshold is exceeded is the point at which the process of change really begins. Until something pushes us over our threshold, we continue to operate within our current way of being. Until that point, no change is necessary because our current way of being can easily deal with whatever happens. Thresholds, as I've explained before, are the points where the old system cannot handle further input from the environment, where it cannot dissipate the necessary entropy and, as a result, becomes more chaotic and begins to break down. Only when the threshold is exceeded does something new become possible. A threshold, then, is a growth point, a moment of truth, and how you handle it determines whether you evolve to the next higher level—or stay the same.

We've all known people who have a low threshold for what they can handle, and as a result are often thrown into emotional turmoil by everyday events, while others seem to be much more resilient and able to cope with whatever happens. Why is this? My view is that when a person is traumatized in some way while growing up, their threshold for what they can handle does not mature in the normal way. Somehow, they're left with a lower threshold than the person who did not suffer such trauma. Such a person's capacity to deal with life's problems has been diminished by their early wounding. They don't handle setbacks, frustrations, difficult people, or disappointments as well as they might had they not suffered traumatic experiences during developmentally sensitive periods in their lives. Research from a variety of sources supports this observation.

In a recent article in *Psychology Today*, "Stress...It's Worse Than You Think," medical writer John Carpi discusses the increased sensitivity to stress some of us experience: ". . . we can become sensitized, or acutely sensitive to stress. Once that happens, even the

Information You Can Use—Every Emotion Has a Chemical Component in the Brain

It's difficult for us to grasp fully the idea that our ideas, our dreams, our values, in fact all of what we consider ourselves to be, whatever else it may be in a spiritual or holistic sense, is in some way the result of electromechanical brain function. Even our ability to empathize with other human beings is a result of this. As Dr. George Lakoff, a cognitive scientist at the University of California at Berkeley, puts it, "Each of us, in the prefrontal cortex of our brains, has what are called 'mirror neurons.' Such neurons fire either when we perform an action or when we see the same action performed by someone else. There are connections from that part of the brain to the emotional centers. Such neural circuits are believed to be the basis of empathy."

http://www.edge.org/documents/whatnow__lakoff.html, (10/18/01)

merest intimation of stress can trigger a cascade of chemical reactions in brain and body that assault us from within."

According to Carpi, everyone has a built-in gauge that controls his or her reaction to stress, a kind of biological thermostat that, when working properly, keeps the body from launching an all-out response, literally over spilled milk. However, according to psychologist Jonathan C. Smith, Ph.D., founder and director of the Stress Institute at Roosevelt University in Chicago, sensitization lowers the thermostat set point.

Support for this claim comes from Seymore Levine, Ph.D., of the University of Delaware, who writes, "Years of research has told us that people do become sensitized to stress and that this sensitization actually alters physical patterns in the brain. That means that once sensitized, the body just does not respond to stress the same way in the future. We may produce too many excitatory chemicals or too few calming ones; either way we are responding inappropriately."

Another researcher, Jean King, Ph.D., of the University of Massachusetts Medical School, believes that when certain stresses occur during developmental periods they may be more damaging than stress suffered at other times: "The psychological events that are most deleterious probably occur during infancy and childhood—an unstable home environment, living with an alcoholic parent, or any other number of extended crises. . . .What we now believe is that a stress of [great] magnitude occurring when you are young may permanently rewire the brain's circuitry, throwing the system askew and leaving it less able to handle normal, everyday stress." (*Psychology Today*, Jan/Feb 1996).

The findings of these scientists mirror my belief, based on years of observing participants in the Centerpointe program, that trauma suffered during the formative years (and occasionally during adulthood, as in the case of Post-Traumatic Stress Disorder) causes a lower threshold for stimulation than if the person had not suffered the trauma.

Because I've seen Holosync raise many people's thresholds, I disagree with Dr. King's contention that the threshold is *permanently* lowered by trauma. I've seen countless Centerpointe participants, who began the program with very low thresholds, raised them, first to normal levels, and eventually, to levels much higher than normal. By the end of the program, they are so mentally and emotionally resilient that very little can pull them off center, despite where they were when they began the program.

In an attempt to cope with the effects of a low threshold, we develop a repertoire of personal coping behaviors as we grow up, along with their accompanying feelings. Coping behaviors and their emotional components include such things as anxiety, confusion, withdrawal, depression, anger, alcohol and drug abuse, overeating, sexual acting out, and many others. They may even include more severe problems, such as personality disorders and psychosis.

What kind of childhood traumas cause lowered thresholds? What does it take to create this sensitivity to one's environment, and the resulting destructive coping strategies? Some traumas are obvious and overt, such as beatings or other forms of physical and verbal abuse. But others are quite subtle. In a thousand ways, large and small, children are given messages (often by loving parents) that have negative psychological consequences. For instance, we've almost all heard the following words or experienced the events that embody these messages. They are an inescapable part of life.

- "Don't try anything new; you might get hurt."
- "Don't put yourself forward like that; you'll probably fail."
- "Don't be naive; people will take advantage of you."
- "Don't have needs; nobody wants to know about them."

- "Don't voice your fears; nobody wants to deal with you unless you're happy and secure."

Of course, these messages are not usually so explicit; they may even leave no memory but still leave a trace in the unconscious mind. Even such subtle traumas can contribute to a lowered threshold.

A New Way to Look at Recovery from Emotional Trauma

Traditional approaches to dealing with problems resulting from past emotional trauma have always seemed to me to be symptom-oriented. The prevailing view in personal development circles is that if you've been traumatized, especially in childhood, you're left with all this detritus buried in the unconscious mind, and this buried emotional garbage is causing problems for you. You are "full of" anger, or "full of" sadness, and these feelings and the accompanying memories need to come to the surface and be "healed." When you can "feel the pain," then you can let it go, the theory goes. This is the basis of many healing programs.

If these approaches are helpful at all, it is in situations where a person has repressed his feelings and memories to such a degree that progress stalls until he become more conscious of them. If there has been a lot of trauma, creating awareness must be done very carefully, usually under the guidance of a skilled therapist. However, just revisiting and re-feeling the pain doesn't heal it. In fact, this reliving of strong emotions and the associated trauma may often re-traumatize the person. Who needs that?

While there are many popular approaches, conventional therapy doesn't really agree on any proven, universally accepted method for getting rid of this supposed detritus of the psyche. But here's my point: it doesn't seem to matter because *there's nothing to flush out of the system anyway.* Instead of trying to get rid of experiences that happened in the past, instead of trying to get rid of emotional "stuff" supposedly buried inside of you, all you really need to do is *raise your threshold.* Then, what used to derail you can't do so anymore. Raising the threshold attacks the problem—sensitivity to stress—at the root, and bypasses the treatment of symptoms, the results of

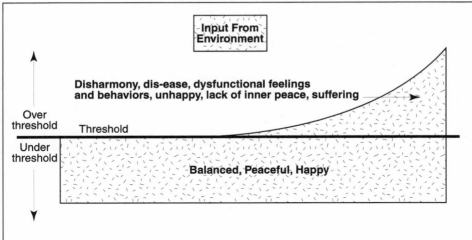

Everyone has a threshold for what they can handle coming at them from their environment (solid horizontal line). If environmental stimuli does not exceed that threshold, we feel balanced, peaceful, and happy. If, however, stimuli become enough that we are pushed over that threshold, we become stressed, and attempt to cope through various dysfunctional feelings and behaviors, including anger, fear, depression, sadness, anxiety, substance abuse, overeating, and many others.

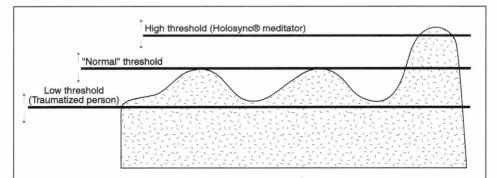

The solid horizontal line on the bottom represents the lower-than-normal threshold of a person who has suffered some sort of trauma. As you can see, this person is chronically over their threshold, and therefore almost constantly stressed and constantly experiencing dysfunctional feelings and behaviors. The horizontal line in the middle represents the threshold of a normal (non-traumatized) person. Though this person's threshold is high enough that most events do not create stress, events can still push this person over their threshold, at which point they, too, experience stress and attempt to cope with dysfunctional feelings and behaviors. The top horizontal line represents the threshold of an experienced Holosync meditator. This person's threshold is high enough that only rarely do events push him over his threshold. For this reason, this person remains peaceful and happy in nearly all situations, dysfunctional feelings and behaviors are very rare, and, if they do occur, they are of greatly diminished intensity.

which are almost always temporary. Then the symptoms—depression, anxiety, fear, anger, substance abuse, self-sabotage, confusion, and many others—evaporate of their own accord.

How the Centerpointe Program Helps You Change

When you begin the Centerpointe program, you have a certain emotional threshold that corresponds to the capacity of your existing brain and nervous system to deal with your environment by dissipating the necessary entropy to keep the system stable. *Awakening Prologue* pushes against that system and pushes the threshold higher. When you finish *Awakening Level 1* (which is really the second level, and the place where we begin to make custom soundtracks), this threshold is higher still. *Awakening Level 2* continues the process, and so on, through all the levels. Eventually, a person's threshold becomes so high that nothing can really disturb their peace of mind.

Long before the end of the program, most dysfunctional feelings and behaviors are gone. I'm not saying you'll never be angry again or never again feel fear or will never again become anxious. There are times when these emotions are appropriate and even healthy. If someone pulls a gun on you, for example, your fear response will mobilize you to protect yourself. There are occasions when anger is normal and helpful in retaining your sense of person-hood. It is also normal to feel temporarily down and depressed as part of the grief process when you've experienced a loss. But these instances differ from dysfunctional responses, which are inappropriate or out of proportion to the occasion. By definition, dysfunctional behavior doesn't work.

You'll find as you move through the Centerpointe program, that your favorite (and generally dysfunctional) coping mechanisms will fall away. As your threshold is pushed higher, it takes more and more stimuli from the environment to trigger them. No longer needed, these coping mechanisms begin to fall away. When you can handle your environment, you feel content, and when you cannot, your old dysfunctional coping mechanisms will come back. Finally, even the times when you *are* pushed over threshold produce only the most minor reactions.

Program participants consistently tell us that as their neurotic and dysfunctional feelings and behaviors fall away, so does the time they spend in suffering mode. Many people have found, for instance, that they no longer need antidepressant medication, sometimes after depending on them for many years. (Of course, always consult your physician before adjusting your medications in any way.) Problems with anger, depression, and anxiety diminish and then disappear, as well as a long list of other complaints. When your system is no longer so easily stressed, you don't need all those defensive overreactions in order to cope.

As the old threshold is pushed higher, a new way of seeing and experiencing emerges. This new way allows one to better handle the ups and downs of the world without needing to deal with them through self-defeating and dysfunctional behaviors, or manifest them as physical and health-related problems. Your brain has "escaped into a higher order," one that embraces more of the connectedness and totality of the universe. And this new ability to handle whatever comes your way creates deep inner peace and happiness.

I'm always cautious when I discuss the emotional aspects of

PERSONAL EXPERIENCE

Like somebody else said, there are definite ups and downs to this system and all meditations. But after almost a year on this system, I can't even compare it to anything else. It's like going from a pony ride to a space shuttle launch. I don't mean to sound overly zealous about it. As well, I'm something of a skeptic in such matters. But I can say that anyone who hasn't tried this system yet is really missing out.

I own a lot of tapes and other stuff which, now, seem pretty wimpy (I gave a bunch of it to my brother to play with!) My roommate in the U.K. got me into this, and I'm still trying to figure out how to repay him. His life has completely turned around as well. His only fault is that he won't shut up about how great the tapes are.

I have had some catharsis, or overwhelm. There were about three days when I thought my brain would just overload. Very much a dark night of the soul experience for me. I had two good cries, and before this I hadn't cried for almost four years. It's like the emotional blinders are off and I can see and breathe again. When I was 20 (I'm 47 now) I had lots of creative energies and inspirations. I thought that was just a nice part about being young. But I'm happy to say that that feeling is back and I feel great. Next week I'm submitting my screenplay to a movie producer. This is something I never thought I'd actually do. Too scared. Plus, I haven't gone to the bottle for eight months now.

—Kurt, *Mind Chatter* No. 6

participating in this program because many of the people who come to us are already experiencing a lot of emotional pain. As I've said before, for most people, most of the time, the experience is very pleasurable, and any periods of discomfort are really the dawning of new and better ways of experiencing life. The program is *not* just one gut-wrenching upheaval after another. Moments of upheaval are the birth pains of greater happiness and inner peace, and as such are worth experiencing. Keeping this in mind will bring things into perspective and make the entire process easier.

I'm convinced that change and personal growth need not be difficult or painful. In the next chapter, I'll talk about how to make the process of change easy. It isn't change that's painful; it's *our resistance to the process* that creates pain. Luckily, there's a very easy-to-administer antidote for this resistance and the pain it creates.

CHAPTER 5

Resistance

I remember sitting in my office one afternoon when e-mails from
four program participants came in at the same time. Their stories
followed the same general pattern: they were using the program
every day and were very pleased with their progress. But all of them
were asking for help in interpreting emotional states they were
experiencing.

One used an analogy to describe the progress she was making.
She pictured herself as a large tree standing in an open field. Hidden
out of sight was an enormous network of roots that solidly anchored
the tree into the ground. Her branches were able to flex and bow in
the wind. She swayed and tossed easily in response to the changing
weather, and she stayed moored to the same spot. Nothing could
blow her over.

But she, like the others I heard from, felt a ripple of unease. An
especially vivid and disturbing dream had returned from her childhood. She dreamed she was stuck in a supposedly normal house that
really had tiny doors and low ceilings. When she tried to walk

forward, the dimensions of the rooms got even smaller, and she couldn't move. As she went through her day, remembering the dream made her uneasy.

Another man told me he was sensitive to noise and was short-tempered when interrupted. He felt on guard all the time, as he used to be before he started the program. When driving, he'd started swearing at other drivers again, and his wife was threatening to do the driving herself if he didn't get a grip on himself.

My third correspondent said he felt an anxiety that he couldn't trace to anything specific; he just felt generally apprehensive. After weeks of feeling free of worry, he was back to stewing about unimportant details. When he first started the program he felt he was making so much progress that his growth was on fast-forward. Now, it felt as if someone had tricked him by pushing the rewind button.

Finally, my last e-mailer just wasn't feeling as physically or mentally well as she normally did. After discarding the idea that she might have a low-level flu, she wondered whether her physical symptoms (low energy, dull headache, muscle aches) could be the result of reaching a threshold. She'd heard me talk about the concept, and she'd read about it in our newsletter, but she wasn't sure if that was what was happening.

I told each of them that, rather than being signs that they were regressing, these were actually signs of progress. It did seem reasonable to conclude that what they were experiencing was a reaction to the program, especially since there were no external reasons for these disturbances. Holosync® was stirring things up emotionally for each of them as it pushed against their individual thresholds. And, like most people, each of them was resisting that push. Though they'd no doubt read my thoughts on resistance, they were failing to apply the general theory to their own specific situation. What they were forgetting is that *all* discomfort, in the final analysis, comes from resistance to whatever is happening. End the resistance, and the discomfort ends, too.

This is a profound statement. It means that it's not *what* you resist that creates discomfort, but rather *the resistance itself*. Think about that for a moment. This means nothing in your environment—no person, no situation—is the cause of your discomfort. This fact gives you power. If situations and people were the cause of our discomfort, we would be at the mercy of whatever was going on around us, and would have to wait for the right conditions to feel good. But because it is our own resistance that creates our discomfort, we can end our discomfort by giving up resistance.

Welcoming the Storm
ⓖ

Let's go back to my four correspondents. Yes, I did think they were approaching the rougher seas that signaled that Holosync was pushing against their individual thresholds in the process of pushing them higher. They were experiencing the temporary symptoms we at Centerpointe call *overwhelm*, a sign that the old system, the old way of being, was at its threshold and going into chaos. Because they identified with the old system, they were resisting its breakdown and subsequent reorganization at a higher level. Because of this resistance, they felt uncomfortable.

People in the Centerpointe program often wish they could predict when a particular bout of upheaval is going to happen, and how long it will last. I wish I could tell them. But each person is different, so each person's path is different. It isn't possible to say, for instance, "At weeks 5, 16, 36, and 78, you'll experience such-and-such symptoms, and they'll last this long." Instead, from the accumulated experience of thousands of participants, we know that most people, just before a leap of growth, will resist the change. And, because of this resistance, they will feel uncomfortable. If they resist a little, the discomfort is minor; if they resist a lot, it can be more intense. If they learn to not resist at all, there is no discomfort at all.

How long these small storms can last varies depending on personal factors relating to the person's emotional history and the way they handle change. Some people have adopted resistance as a major life strategy (I, for instance, was one of these), while others are more able to go with the flow. Anyone, however, can learn to spot the signs of impending change and actually welcome them, rather than resist.

Resistance and Safety
ⓖ

Let's revisit the reason why we would resist in the first place: when we're growing up, we create an internal and largely unconscious model of who we are and how we fit in to and relate to the rest of the world. Our unconscious goal is to create the *greatest feeling of safety* in our family situation. Because the world outside our family often has very different dynamics, this model doesn't usually work as well outside our family. When we deal with people and situations in the outside world the same way we dealt with our family, it often creates problems. You may have learned to ignore your mother when she nagged you, because when you did this she eventually left you alone, but this might not be the best strategy with your boss. You may have been afraid to share sad feelings with your father, because he was unsympathetic and criticized you for having them, but to do the same with your husband may keep you from experiencing the closeness and intimacy you want.

When we recognize these problems as adults, we may seek to make changes in ourselves, running off to the bookstore or the therapist's office (or to Centerpointe). At the same time, on an unconscious level, we strongly associate the old way of being with safety. Consciously, we may ardently want the changes, but unconsciously, they make us afraid. When the chips are down, this unconscious part is more powerful than our conscious will-power and can create tremendous resistance. And the greater the lack of physical or emotional safety in our family, the more we cling to the old behaviors and feelings that helped us survive in that situation. In such a case, changing our carefully constructed model of reality can feel *very* unsafe, and our resistance to doing so can be very strong.

Though most resistance is unconscious, we've still found at Centerpointe that a conscious understanding of the process is helpful. When people realize, at least theoretically, that the chaos they fear is the prelude to positive change, it sometimes helps them relax. When they're able to look at the process as a continual cycle of death and rebirth, and remember that the cycle is painful only when they identify with what is dying, it often eases their distress. It's also helpful to realize that feeling unsafe does not mean you really *are* unsafe. When we can look around us and see, objectively, that there's nothing unsafe happening at that moment in our environment, we can actually learn to associate the unsafe feeling with the idea that *something better is coming*, rather than feeling *this is dangerous*. In that case, we can learn to welcome it as just a part of the change process.

The Unholy Trinity of Resistance

All of us have developed dysfunctional or self-defeating behaviors that we use to try to cope with unpleasant or stressful experiences. One of the reasons people join the Centerpointe program in the first place is because they don't like the consequences of their destructive coping mechanisms. They've learned to rely on these old habits and reactions for comfort and protection, and hang onto them even when it becomes apparent that they're a major cause of suffering and pain—a great example of the cure being worse than the disease.

The association between what we perceive to be a problem and the strategy that helps us cope with it is very strong. For example, a grown daughter might find herself drinking more during a visit from her mother. A man might withdraw from social contact in the face of mounting financial pressures. A student might seek escape in romance novels instead of facing the challenge of her calculus homework. The problem with these ways of coping is that they take on lives of their own. Once they become common behavior patterns, you have the additional problems generated by the way you've chosen to cope with the first problem.

At Centerpointe, we've identified three common dysfunctional strategies for dealing with being pushed over threshold. Because these strategies are largely unconscious, becoming aware of which of them you use can be very valuable. As you become more aware of them, you'll find that they begin to lose their hold on you.

Dissipating Energy. This is the frantic attempt to dissipate the extra input your system can't handle. What's coming at you exceeds your current ability to dissipate the necessary entropy, and as this entropy builds up inside you, you frantically try to push it out, as if bailing a sinking boat. Common examples of dissipating energy are strenuous physical exercise, sexual activity, and even talking. More extreme forms are crying, compulsive behaviors, and anger. Anything that pushes energy out of the system fits this general category. This strategy turns frustration outward.

The main problem with this strategy is that, while it may temporarily relieve the pressure, it doesn't allow the entropy to build up to the point where it pushes the system to reorganize at a higher level,

Three Ways People Deal with Overwhelm

1.   **Dissipating Energy**

High input from environment   System cannot dissipate entropy

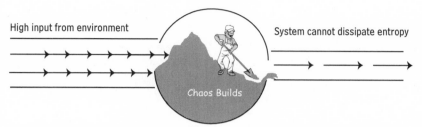

Chaos Builds

Some people when stressed or overwhelmed try to frantically push the entropy out through anger, crying, physical activity, sex, talking or anything else that pushes energy out of the system and relieves the pressure

2.   **Blocking Energy**

High input from environment   System cannot dissipate entropy

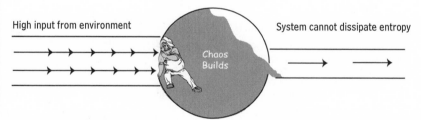

Chaos Builds

Others will do anything they can to keep more from entering the system by isolating themselves, shutting down, becoming depressed, or even becoming ill

3.   **Distraction**

High input from environment

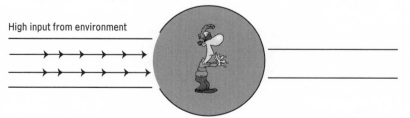

Usually while using one of the two strategies above, people will also distract themselves with alcohol, drugs, sex, TV, activity, reading, etc.

raising your threshold. Your ability to handle more input without overwhelm never improves because the system that makes up who you are never changes. As you push the extra entropy out of the system, you may feel temporary relief. But because the threshold remains the same, the next time you are stimulated in the same way, you will once again be overwhelmed in the same way—and, you will react (and suffer) in the same way. Your extra effort to push the entropy out of the system does not deal with the root cause of the problem, which is that your threshold is too low to handle the environment you're in.

In our society, anger is the primary way people try to cope, and is the most common response to being pushed past one's emotional threshold. As a result, program participants who are prone to anger may find themselves angry or irritated from time to time as Holosync pushes against their threshold, just as a weight lifter might experience sore muscles each time he adds more weight to his routine. Once the threshold has been pushed high enough by the Holosync stimulus, however, the anger and other destructive behaviors fall

Centerpointe Insight—Depression and Holosync

We've probably received more feedback from participants regarding relief from depression than from any other condition. Many people report being able to discontinue depression medication after as little as 10 to 12 months in the program. (Depression medication is necessary in some situations. Never discontinue medication without consulting your doctor.) Here are a few comments we've received regarding Holosync and depression:

"I was on anti-depressant and anti-anxiety pills for 10 years. After doing Holosync for one and a half years, I was able to stop taking the medication completely. But of course, I took the medication for one day and stop taking for two days. I followed this schedule for two months before I was able to completely stop. I can tell you that Holosync is the reason why I was able to break free. Before using Holosync, I tried this method, but was not successful. I tried a few times, in fact. I felt confusion and nausea and was even more depressed and anxious. Though I still have lots of c—p to resolve, I am happy because I don't need this medication anymore."

—Jan Y.

"I had been depressed for many years, ranging from the 'blues' to 'for God's sake go and get some help.' It's difficult to know how serious one's depression is because it's only your own that you know, but I think mine certainly reached the major stage, as you describe it, perhaps beyond that too. I mean, there were times I'd liked to have killed myself.

"Never took drugs or sought any kind of counseling help. I knew there was a way through it and that wasn't the road for me. It was difficult to sweat it out, though, with so much well meaning advice from friends. Came across Holosync, seemingly by accident, and bought it on instinct. It felt right. It's difficult to put into words the effect it had. I immediately began to feel better, much better—in fact, happy even—and have never looked back. Now on Awakening Level 3 and, while it would be foolish to say the depression will never return, I really can't imagine it will, because that strategy no longer seems relevant. It's almost as if I couldn't be bothered to be depressed anymore."

—Robert

"I've been doing Holosync since the end of '99. Before that I was suffering from quite severe depression. Since then, I occasionally get a bit down but nothing I can't handle. I had already chosen not to take any more anti-depressants after a brief spell of happiness in '98. Holosync enables you to look rationally at your problems [and] put perspective on deeply rooted fears and anxiety."

—"Nimbus"

"I'd been depressed for over a year before I started Holosync. I'd been on the drugs from the Doc. These simply made me not mind being depressed, useless rotten things—I hate anti-depressants. Thoughts of a couple of bottles of whisky and bottles of aspirin on the beach were dominating my mind more and more just nine weeks ago. I even got preoccupied with timing the tides!

"Within a week of starting Holosync, I began to feel a lot better; within three weeks I felt great. The only remnants of depression that I have now is that I still can't watch the news because every time I see pictures of starving and sick children I lose it emotionally. My reaction to most stuff is normal again (my normal). I would recommend Holosync to anyone with depression—it's a lot healthier than the drugs and you actually get better instead of mask the symptoms. I can't imagine anyone getting worse with Holosync. I'm a regular relaxation junky now and it's doing me the world of good."

—Paula

away. You use these behaviors only when you are *over* your threshold, and once the threshold is high enough to handle what's going on in your life, dysfunctional behaviors become unnecessary.

Blocking Energy. The second category of coping mechanisms are behaviors that try to block additional energy from entering an overloaded system. They include a desire to isolate or, in more extreme cases, as depression. In depression, we shut down metabolically, we breathe less, and we even unconsciously constrict the pupils of our eyes so as to take in less light. We want to be alone and to get away from any kind of input. Other behaviors that attempt to block additional incoming energy include loss of appetite and some forms of illness. With this strategy, frustration turns inward.

Though attempts to block or reduce input can give the system a chance to rest and dissipate the overload, the end result is the same as with the strategies for frantically dissipating energy: the system remains the same instead of evolving to a higher level. As with the first strategy, the next time the system is stimulated in the same way, you'll again react with the same upset and suffering.

Distraction. The third strategy is to indulge in anything that draws attention away from the problem. Excessive use of drugs, alcohol, sex, television, spacing out, eating, and perhaps even more severe strategies such as personality disorders and psychosis—all of these distract or deaden you to what's happening, and are attempts to ignore the feeling of overwhelm. You feel the growing internal chaos as your system approaches the evolutionary moment of truth, and it's uncomfortable. Distraction is one way to mitigate the discomfort. It's also the least effective of the three strategies because it doesn't even give the old, inadequate system a chance to regroup.

It's common for people to use one of the first two methods as a primary coping mechanism, followed closely by the other as a backup. Some people react first with anger, and then, if pushed further, withdraw or become depressed. Others withdraw or get depressed first, and then react with anger if pushed further. Often method number three, distraction, operates in the background the whole time. We use these strategies because they work to a certain extent, at least in the short run. There is some temporary release of pressure, and we might feel better for a while, but no real evolution takes place because the system is never allowed to reach the point of peak experience where it spontaneously reorganizes itself.

In 1985, when I began using Holosync soundtracks to meditate,

Q & A—
Will my life be perfect after completing the Centerpointe program?

There is no magic bullet that will make everything in your life perfect. Life is filled with problems—for everyone. When Tom Hanks was asked what it was like to be "at the top of the heap," he said, "No matter where you are on the heap, life is one thing after another." He's right.

What our program does is allow you to live with greater awareness, which allows you to drop automatic, unconscious responses that create suffering. Instead, you'll have *choice* responses. The program helps you respond to things that once made you mad, depressed, anxious, or afraid, with the attitude of "so what?" You remain happy, peaceful, and centered regardless of what's going on around you.

Different annoying and painful things happen to everyone; the difference is in how you respond to them. I can't tell you how much different my life is since I went through the Centerpointe program. Now I *never* get depressed, where before I was depressed quite often. I rarely get angry now, and before I completed the program I used to be angry constantly. I rarely feel afraid anymore. Now, whenever these responses occur (which is rarely), I get out of them in just a few moments because I now have a choice of how to feel or behave. Before the program I was, like most people, really nothing but an automatic response mechanism.

Do all kinds of things still happen in my life? Yes. Are they the same things that used to drive me crazy, make me angry, depress me, and so on? Yes. Do they affect me in the same way now? No. Did that change my life? Immeasurably. Will the same thing happen for you? Absolutely.

my favorite coping mechanism was anger, closely followed by depression. As I write this, depression and anger are no longer part of my life. I certainly am capable of feeling down or irritated—temporarily—but the feelings are moderate, and I know what I can do to get rid of them. My threshold for what I can handle is now so high that very little bothers me anymore. The coping mechanisms I learned while growing up have fallen away through disuse.

Being a Good Child Can Make You an Unhappy Adult

⑥

There's no doubt that some people have a harder time adjusting to change than others. These people emerge from childhood with a legacy that leaves them short-changed—a lower threshold for what they can handle. Part of this lower threshold is tied to certain attitudes we adopt during childhood. One of the most debilitating of these is what Dr. Al Siebert has called *the good child syndrome*.

Have you spent a lifetime "shoulding" on yourself, looking around and seeing other people doing things you "can't" do—making this kind of money; being this kind of husband, wife, or lover; being this kind of father, son, mother, or daughter; or doing exciting or unusual things? You say, "I should be doing that too. I should be this kind of person; I shouldn't be that kind." You want to be "a good child," even as an adult. This may be such an ingrained part of your life that you do it automatically, unconsciously. Maybe you *should* make a list of all the things you "should" do, and examine whether you really want to do them.

To be fair, when you've treated someone badly, you feel sorry and this should cause you to stop doing similar things. But that's different from responding to what authority figures in your past have planted in your mind about who you should or should not be. At Centerpointe we believe in doing something because it's possible, and because we want to do it (because we like and desire the consequences of doing it), not because our programming tells us it's necessary. If you aren't doing something in your life, we want it to be because you don't want the consequences, not because you shouldn't be doing it. If you frequently feel guilty, it may be because you decide what to do based on whether or not you "should" do it. If you're frequently frustrated, you may be doing many things because you "have to," not because you want to.

A good child is someone who has learned to follow the rules, but in many situations the rule follower, the good child, doesn't have many options. The good child is rule bound and must act a certain way, thereby limiting his flexibility. Living by the rules gives you a planned way of dealing with life and removes uncertainty about what to do in a given situation (at least that's the theory), but it's constricting. Since no set of rules can handle every situation, you will often find yourself feeling helpless and at a loss as to what to do, or angry

80

because the world is not following the "should" script that you were taught to expect. When you build your life on rules instead of by responding flexibly to real-life, real-time information, the results can be pretty miserable.

Part of the problem is that most good-child messages come in the form of prohibitions—what parents want their child *not* to become or *not* do. They use people they consider to be bad as anti-models of how to behave and think they must wring from their child all traces of bad ways of thinking, feeling, and acting. Unfortunately, efforts to create a good child often produce an adult who copes poorly with life—or an adult hypocrite.

Raising A Good Child*		
What a Parent Wants to Say	**What a Child Hears**	**How the Good Child Acts as an Adult**
A good child is one who is:	To be a good child:	To be a good adult:
Not negative	Don't talk back.	Fear being regarded as hurtful, tough, selfish, insensitive or uncaring.
Not angry	Be polite.	
Not selfish	Stop pouting.	
Not dishonest	Be neat.	Smile when upset.
Not self-centered or prideful	Don't whine.	Deny anger.
	Don't hit.	Don't make selfish requests.
Not rebellious	Don't fight.	
	Stop complaining.	Tell people things for their own good.
	Smile no matter what.	Give "should" instructions to others.
	Don't cry.	Say critical things behind other's backs.
	Stop asking questions.	
	Don't be stuck-up.	Alert and warn others about "bad" people.
	Don't be angry.	Don't accept compliments easily. When hurting others say, "But I mean well."
	Don't be selfish.	

*Adapted from The Survivor Personality, *by Al Siebert. New York, NY: Berkeley Pub. Group, 1996.*

Being the good child has nothing to do with age. Some people in their eighties are still bound by rules taught to them in childhood, and when they do something outside the rules, they feel guilty and uneasy. When someone else breaks their rules, they become angry or depressed. How uncomfortable do you feel when you step outside the rules you were taught early in life? Does it make sense to you to eat everything on your plate because your parents taught you to, even though you're feeling full, are overweight, and have been warned by your doctor to cut back on calories? Are there rules you still keep, despite their lack of value in your life? It's important to let go of the concept of who you "should" be. If you're conscious of this, you'll stop worrying about it. One of the goals of the Centerpointe program is to create in participants what Dr. Al Siebert calls the *survivor personality*.

Developing Resilience
⑥

Acting as the good child makes a person vulnerable to being overwhelmed when faced with challenges to which their rules don't apply, or which are beyond the limits of the act they were trained to perform. Therefore, the good child will resist change, both consciously and unconsciously. The challenge for someone raised to be good is to develop new ways of thinking, feeling, and acting. This requires courage because it requires stepping outside the artificial shell of goodness into what may seem to be risky, and even frightening, territory.

Dr. Siebert, author of *The Survivor Personality*, has spent his professional life studying *resiliency*. He has interviewed prisoners of war, kidnap victims, and rape victims in order to discover why some people are resilient while others aren't. Resiliency, he concluded, can be learned, but it can't be taught. Paradoxically, if you teach someone "the rules" for being resilient, and they attempt to follow them, they cannot become resilient. Resilient people are not rule bound. Instead, they deal with each situation with a flexible approach that allows them to choose the most resourceful way to be or behave in that situation. They respond to the world based on the outcomes and consequences they want, rather than on whatever rules they were taught by parents, teachers, friends, the media, and the general culture. This gives them an ability to deal with whatever happens

PERSONAL EXPERIENCE

It seems like yesterday (2 1/2 years ago) that I started Centerpointe. It has been quite a journey for me, as life is for anyone with a burning desire to be all they can be. I would summarize the program as "turning the volume up in life."

Nothing is dramatically different in my life except for me! I no longer rush to be someone, somewhere, by sometime, and choose instead to get the most out of every moment, which equates to living life to the full. I have been through so many ups and downs over the last few years that I no longer strive for extremes but simply take situations as they come.

I have become more intelligent and successful in my IT career, able to lead people and create ideas in ways never dreamed of; more confident speaking and communicating; I sleep less, etc., etc....

Centerpointe is frighteningly accurate in its portrayal of what you will get out of the program and the process, so far. All you have to do is be open to what they are trying to say and read *Mind Chatter*, which I regularly look forward to.

—David W., *Mind Chatter* No. 62

with a much wider and more flexible repertoire of options and strategies.

Not surprisingly, people who are resilient have many seemingly opposing, flexible patterns. They don't have to obey all the rules all the time and can adopt one posture or point of view in one situation, and the opposite posture or point of view in another. There is no inner voice in them that says that rules are more important than success, survival—or happiness.

They are both kind *and* selfish. They can be deceptive *and* honest. They can be open *and* guarded. They have a paradoxical, two-sides-of-the-same-coin collection of traits, such as selfish-unselfish, pessimist-optimist, sensitive-tough, strong-gentle, and distant-friendly. They have *emotional* flexibility, and because of it they can flow with what's happening much more easily than those who do not. They realize that each response has consequences and they behave accordingly. They do not need rules to decide what to do or to evaluate what they've done. They evaluate what is happening and what to do by the moment-to-moment consequences.

For example, being dishonest may be truly honest in certain situations. If you are a kidnap victim, it might make sense to obey some of the rules of the captor in order to stay alive. But in order for a resilient prisoner to stay alive, he or she will undoubtedly compromise many rules, including the internalized rules of "nice" behavior.

Unfortunately, as I said, a flexible, resilient personality cannot be taught, although it can be modeled. Resiliency is not a new act designed to replace the old one. It is, rather, the emergence of innate abilities made possible by learning from experience and responding flexibly to whatever is happening.

Like most people, I used to be a good child, and seeing myself as a good child in need of resiliency was a revelation to me. And though the intellectual understanding was important, it was using the Centerpointe program that finally created the shift that took me from my inflexible good-boy charade to the more real and more flexible place I'm in today. This shift has brought me happiness, inner peace, the ability to get along with people, and success in the world. I now have the ability to thrive in any situation. Ironically, I feel as if I'm genuinely good today, without trying to be.

What You Can Do
⑥

First, let me say that I'm not advocating anarchism, or saying that not being rule-bound means you should just do whatever you want. Instead, I'm saying that in each situation, instead of checking the rules, the resilient person evaluates the consequences and then acts. Being resilient is the opposite of being an automatic response mechanism. When you run on automatic, the consequences are often not what you anticipated or wanted. And when you run on automatic, you often end up in resistance. Operating with resiliency, however, makes life easy.

Let's get back, then, to the problem of resistance and how to deal with it. Since resistance is the cause of all discomfort, finding a way to eliminate it changes everything and ends any suffering you've been creating for yourself.

The problem, as most people see it, is that resistance just seems to *happen*. You don't consciously decide to resist, you just do it automatically when something happens you don't like. Ironically, trying to control everything is the root of the problem.

It's when you stop trying to control resistance that it goes away. That is the secret. Let me repeat it: It's when you stop trying to control it that it goes away.

First, you have to recognize that there *is* resistance. You do this by noticing when you're experiencing discomfort. Discomfort = resistance, every time. No exceptions. *All discomfort—in the Center-pointe program and in life in general—is a result of being over your threshold and then resisting that fact.* When you feel discomfort, notice it: "There I am, feeling _____. I must be in resistance." Then *watch* yourself. Notice how your body feels; notice your thoughts, notice your emotions. Just *notice*.

Approach whatever you're experiencing, whether it's pleasant or unpleasant, with curiosity. Let it be okay that whatever is happening is happening. Just watch. Pretend that you're a scientist who's been lurking in the Amazon jungle for the past 25 years, searching for a certain butterfly—when you finally spot one, you're not going to miss a thing. When one finally appears, you're keenly interested and curious to just watch and notice what happens.

I know this instruction may seem simplistic, even nonsensical. "Deal with all those times when I'm suffering by just *noticing them?!*" I promise, however, that if you can treat your upheaval in this manner, most of it will disappear *immediately*. This is especially true if you're not trying to make it disappear (which, of course, is just more resistance).

If this observer role is new to you, you might not do it very well at first, but you'll get better at it as you practice. As you master being the watcher of what happens, you'll be amazed at how much more easily you'll be able to handle what comes. Once you realize that all discomfort is created by resistance to "what is," the obvious solution is to let what is be okay and to not fight against it. One powerful way to do this is to step back and just watch, and once you do that, the discomfort, the suffering, stops. I'll go much more deeply into this idea of watching in the next chapter.

If you're watching yourself in this way whenever you feel discomfort, and you're still having trouble while using the Centerpointe program (which just means you haven't yet mastered being the watcher), then it's time to take a vacation from the tapes or CDs until your nervous system catches up. In that case, take a day off. Take two days off if need be. If your muscles were sore from too much running, you'd probably take a day off from your physical training. Discomfort and upheaval in this program are the sore muscles of spiritual growth.

Upheaval is part of life, and if you're on a path of growth, you'll experience more of it than if you hide from growth. When you resist upheaval as it occurs, you suffer. When you let it be okay, however, you may feel *intensity*, but you will not suffer over it. Though the intensity may remain, it will be *neutral* intensity rather than negative intensity.

Many experiences in life have intensity, and this intensity can be positive, negative, or neutral, depending on whether we welcome it, resist it, or are ambivalent toward it. Most people assume the quality of intensity they feel in a given situation is intrinsic to that experience, but it's actually a result of the *meaning* they place on the experience. For that reason, an intense experience, if it isn't resisted, may still be intense, but not in a negative way.

Learning how to not resist what happens will bring you freedom, happiness, inner peace. It allows you to *choose* your response in any given situation, based on what is best for you and the world around you.

It may take you a while to learn how to let whatever happens be okay. Since this is the case, I want you to be secure in the fact that no

Centerpointe Insight—Reducing Overwhelm

Here are some simple techniques to help you manage overwhelm.

First, do some moderate and regular physical exercise. Because some people tend toward obsessive behaviors when experiencing discomfort, be careful not to overdo it. You don't need to spend three hours on the treadmill. Just do enough to get your heart rate up a little and get your respiratory system going strong.

Many people store tension physically, and exercise can be a good way to minimize this physical tension. Tension can lead to physical illness unless released, and exercise is a natural and healthy way to do that. In addition, the brain creates endorphins during exercise, which can make you feel better emotionally, too.

We also highly recommend hatha yoga. Yoga is ideal for meditators, and was, in fact, developed to help meditators deal with the changes that accompany spiritual growth.

Second, do some deep breathing exercises. One of the simplest and most effective breathing techniques is the cleansing breath. Stand with feet flat on the floor. Take a deep breath in through the nose, filling the diaphragm first, then the lungs. Take a big breath, but don't strain to inhale. Hold the breath for just a moment, two or three seconds, then release the breath in one big rush, like a balloon deflating.

Do this three or four times, at least twice a day. An ideal time is right before your Holosync listening session. Never underestimate the power of breathing. With proper breathing we can regulate the metabolism, provide the brain with adequate oxygen, and flush toxins from the system. So when experiencing overwhelm, the old adage is good advice: take a nice, deep breath!

The third technique is to be creative. Even if you're not artistic, engaging in artwork, without attachment to the result, can be very therapeutic. And if you are artistic, try doing something you aren't already talented at doing. If you're a poet, don't write a poem, and if you paint, don't draw a picture. Do something that you won't need to critique, something that approaches play but which exercises some of your creative muscles.

Don't try, necessarily, to create something of artistic value. In fact, your plan should be to throw away whatever you make. Be focused on the process, not the product.

These techniques—moving, breathing, creating—can help you cope with overwhelm and can sometimes expedite the process of mental and emotional healing and release. They also keep you from falling into dysfunctional strategies you've used before. Above all, keep one important truth in mind: overwhelm, too, will pass. It isn't chronic. It will go away with time. When it does, you'll feel as others who have gone through it before you have felt: more centered, calmer, and with more mental clarity, than before.

matter how much you may resist, the Centerpointe program will eventually push you through it. Resistance can make the program uncomfortable, but it won't keep it from working. Also, when it happens, let it be okay that you're experiencing discomfort. Don't expect to master resistance instantly (though it is possible). And I'm not saying you should *like* the fact that you're experiencing resistance and discomfort. Simply being okay with it means acknowledging it, being present with it, and making your peace with the fact that it is the experience you are having. Experiencing discomfort also doesn't mean that you are doing something wrong, or that you're a failure. The most advanced meditators experience overwhelm. It is a natural part of meditation and personal growth.

At the same time, don't go looking for it. Many people make the mistake of thinking that growth can't happen without discomfort. In personal growth, "no pain, no gain" is *not* the rule. If you can elimi-nate your resistance by noting it and letting it go, the discomfort will disappear. It's just that for most of us it's not so easy to eliminate all the resistance because a lot of it is unconscious. So don't spend a lot of energy preparing for overwhelm. It may or may not occur. If it does, don't worry. In the big picture, discomfort isn't really that bad.

Also keep in mind what I said at the beginning of this chapter: we resist change when it doesn't feel safe. This means that the part of you that doesn't feel safe needs reassurance that things will be better once the change takes place. Though it may sound trite, you can have a talk with that part of yourself, and tell it that you will make sure that all changes you make will be safe.

A Bigger Picture
⑥

In every area of contemporary life—family, sexuality, race rela-tions, religion, government, economics, technology, the environment, personal psychology, and spirituality—old systems are breaking down as they prepare to reorganize at higher levels. In every one of these areas we can either collapse into chaos or move forward in the hope that we will make the leap to the next evolutionary level. Most of us really don't realize just how good we can feel, how good life can be. We can't find satisfaction living out our lives as automatic re-sponse mechanisms, always unconsciously on guard to protect ourselves from dangers that remind us of, or in some ways reopen, our childhood wounds. We also can't find satisfaction by continually and automatically scanning our environment to discover the appli-cable rules, or to notice who's not following them. Acting as an automatic response mechanism when pushed past our threshold for what we can handle is more frightening and miserable, by far, than anything we might encounter during the adventure of discovery, healing, and unfolding made possible by Holosync technology.

Resistance has been such a constant companion for most of us that we can't quite conceive of living without it. I can honestly tell you, however, that it's not only possible to live without resistance, it's much preferable. Resistance, as far as I can tell, serves no useful purpose, unless you like suffering. In the next chapter I'll discuss some other tools and some ways of looking at reality that can help you move forward to make the changes you want to make and become the magnificent person I know you're capable of being.

PERSONAL EXPERIENCE

It has been one year ago today since I began listening to the Holosync tapes. About six weeks into *Awakening Prologue*, I started to experience some upheaval, which manifested itself mostly as anger and depression. Once it passed, I had more anger, but it gradually subsided until, last month, it practically disappeared. These past 6 weeks have been some of the best I have ever experienced in my entire life. I have a calmness and understanding of life that is totally new to me, and quite welcome, I must say. Something has changed about the way I feel about life that I just can't explain, but I feel so comfortable that I'm sure that everything will just get progressively better.

Many of the experiences Bill Harris told me about in the beginning have happened. Even though the first 10 1/2 months were very trying at times, I wouldn't trade them for anything I can think of. Sometimes the upheaval left me feeling like life was futile, but I hung in and let the tapes do their magic. I feel more happy and friendly than I have felt in a very long time. A lot of cynicism has left me and I'm feeling more positive about my future and the life I am living. At present, I am working toward making several changes in my professional and personal life. Centerpointe has changed my life to one of confidence and no fear. By the way, I am 48 years old.

It is a welcome relief to finally find a system that really works as profoundly as the Holosync tapes. I just want to thank Bill Harris and the entire Centerpointe Institute for the new life you have helped me acquire, and I am only about 12% through the program. I am presently at *Awakening Level 2* and have already ordered *Level 3*. I intend to complete the entire course. With all the progress I have made, I just can't imagine where I'll be in the years to come, but it's bound to be wonderful.

—Michael C., *Mind Chatter* No. 5

THERE'S A ZEN STORY OF AN ENLIGHTENED DISCIPLE OF A GREAT ENLIGHTENED MASTER WHO, UPON HEARING OF HIS MASTER'S DEATH, BEGAN TO CRY UNCONTROLLABLY. HIS FOLLOWERS WERE SHOCKED TO SEE HIM CRY. "WHY ARE YOU CRYING? YOU'RE ENLIGHTENED. YOU'RE SUPPOSED TO BE BEYOND SUFFERING. WHAT WILL PEOPLE THINK?"

HE COMPOSED HIMSELF AS BEST HE COULD, AND TURNING TO THEM SAID, "WHAT CAN I DO? MY EYES ARE CRYING. THEY'RE SO SAD THAT THEY WILL NEVER AGAIN SEE THIS TEACHER I LOVED SO MUCH."

CHAPTER 6

Conscious Living

As the above story so poignantly points out, the sorrow of loss is a normal part of being human. This is true even if you are an enlightened master and supposedly not subject to desires and attachments and the suffering they can create. Humans are hard-wired to experience a whole range of feelings and emotions. These feelings and emotions are normal, but suffering over them is not necessary, nor is it desirable. Let me explain what I mean by this baffling, and apparently contradictory, statement.

The Four Noble Truths of Buddhism point out that all life involves suffering (Noble Truth No. 1), that suffering is caused by desire or attachment (Nobel Truth No. 2), and that suffering can be ended by giving up attachment (Nobel Truth No. 3). The 4th Noble Truth is the Buddhist method of giving up attachment.

The Four Nobel Truths are based on an obvious, fundamental, but often overlooked reality of human existence: *all things exist "in time" and eventually pass away.* It's pretty obvious that *not* getting what

The Four Noble Truths	
Noble Truth No. 1	**All life is suffering.**
Noble Truth No. 2	**Suffering is caused by attachment to certain outcomes or results.**
Noble Truth No. 3	**Suffering can be ended by giving up attachment.**
Noble Truth No. 4	**The Buddhist method for learning how to give up attachment.**

you want (or getting what you *don't* want) involves suffering, but it is equally true that *getting what you want* also involves suffering. This is because the thing you want is, like everything else, transitory. This month you're Employee of the Month, but next month you aren't. You love playing with your baby daughter, but she'll grow up. You're alive now, but someday you'll die. If you're attached to these things not changing, you will suffer.

I vividly remember the first time I experienced this truth. I was four years old, and my mother had bought me an ice cream cone. As I began licking the ice cream, I was in heaven. But half way through, the realization hit me that this wonderful experience was going to end. While I certainly enjoyed the rest, the experience was tainted by the fact that I knew the ice cream would soon be gone. Even at the tender age of four, in the midst of my pleasure, I suffered.

It's never too early to learn that being attached to particular outcomes (even one as minor as an ice cream cone lasting forever) causes pain and suffering. And yet, we're trained to believe that happiness is tied to specific events or, especially in our culture, to specific things. Messages all around us connect positive emotions to the things we do and own. The children playing with this year's hot toys are *happy*. The man and woman standing beside their new car are *in love*. The family members sitting around the dinner table eating canned pasta sauce are *united in their humor and affection*. The woman just given the diamond is *young and beautiful*.

Because we live in a mass culture where meaning is centralized, we're used to having others interpret our lives for us. We have, in many cases, become passive observers of our own experience, waiting for other people to tell us what it means. Outside influences so often direct our attention to what we should care about or strive for that the truth of our own power to choose escapes us.

You Are the Author and the Artist
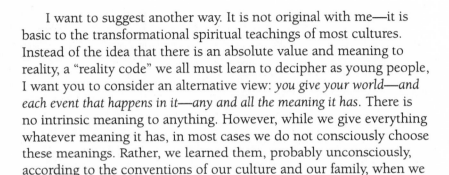

I want to suggest another way. It is not original with me—it is basic to the transformational spiritual teachings of most cultures. Instead of the idea that there is an absolute value and meaning to reality, a "reality code" we all must learn to decipher as young people, I want you to consider an alternative view: *you give your world—and each event that happens in it—any and all the meaning it has.* There is no intrinsic meaning to anything. However, while we give everything whatever meaning it has, in most cases we do not consciously choose these meanings. Rather, we learned them, probably unconsciously, according to the conventions of our culture and our family, when we

Centerpointe Insight—Being Awake

You cannot be otherwise than at one with everything. Everything in the universe is connected in a giant matrix of energy and matter. You don't need to take my word for this, since physicists have been saying the same thing for decades. It is, therefore, a mistaken impression that you are separate. That's why they call the discovery of who and what you really are self-*realization*. It's not that you achieve something when you become awakened—you just come to realize what is already true.

In fact, one way to look at this whole subject would be to say that when your attachments become preferences, it happens because you begin to know, experientially, that you are one with everything. Knowing that you are one with everything, you don't have to be attached to anything (it would be like being attached to your leg—it's already you, and you don't have to do anything to make it be more you than it already is). Instead, you realize that the unfolding of the universe is happening in its own way and is being guided by something much bigger than you. All you have to do is go along for the ride—kind of like white water rafting. So here's my description of being spiritually awake. The awake person is not at odds with the world. He is a part of it, but not attached to the outcome. Like Jesus, he is "in the world but not of it." He watches as it all goes by, but he is also a participant. He knows most people are caught in the world but unaware of being caught, so he is compassionate, and does what he can to help others with their suffering.

To him, the world is a play, and life is like playing a part in that play. He knows it's just a role, but he plays it to the hilt, and enjoys every moment. But he also realizes that the script is just a script, and from the highest perspective it doesn't matter what part has been written for him. He exerts a certain amount of control over his part, but ultimately has only limited influence over what is, because his effort is just one of an infinite number of other efforts, all with their own ends in mind.

Instead of being an automatic response mechanism, responding to the world based on unconscious rules, beliefs, fears, and limitations, he is able to consciously evaluate each situation, in the moment, and instantly and instinctively know exactly what to do and how to respond in order to gain the most resourceful outcome, both for himself and for others.

Mainly, he watches as he plays his part and marvels at the complexity, the infinite permutations, the surprises, the certainties, and the uncertainties. He is calm most of the time, but sometimes his part requires him to be upset or to have some other emotion or reaction. That is being human. But whatever his mood, there is an underlying peace of mind, an underlying, effortless happiness.

You can be this way, too. It doesn't happen overnight, but it can happen. Using the Centerpointe program isn't the only way it can happen, but it's a very good and very fast way.

were children. These prepackaged meanings can have a tremendous influence on how we experience the world, because how we feel about any given thing is directly related to the meaning it has for us. The great news is that we're not stuck with any particular meaning. We can consciously choose the meaning and value of our experiences. This is exactly what people who are continually happy and peaceful have learned to do, and you can learn to do it, too.

This means, of course, that you are the creator of your own reality. In contrast to how you may have been conditioned to think, *you* assign meaning and significance to whatever happens to you, though the process may be unconscious. Then, based on that meaning, you choose (again, usually unconsciously) what your response will be. This principle has a corollary: *you* will *make wise and resource-*

ful choices to the extent that *you live consciously rather than unconsciously*. If, like most people, the part of you that assigns meaning runs on automatic, it will choose meanings and responses based on your cultural, societal, familial, and species background. In that case, you are not exercising your ability to create what you want, and you will have to accept the consequences of these culturally assigned meanings. Your individuality and creativity will remain stillborn. What is more, you will spend a lot of time suffering.

If, on the other hand, you are able to wake up and become more aware of what moves and motivates you, you will see that *you* have picked up the paintbrush; *you* are painting the shapes of your feelings on that blank canvas. Because you are the artist and the author, you can paint anything you like. What you are painting is as ephemeral as anything else in life, but the lines you draw, the shapes you form, and the colors you choose are what give your life meaning. While we are all influenced by the cultural and personal settings in which we live, some people find independence, becoming artists who can express the dictates of their own heart; others become proponents of schools run by others.

The implications of finding independence and being the artist of your own life are staggering. Here is one of them: because you create the world you inhabit, *pain and suffering really can be optional*. Only when you acknowledge your role in your life—and understand your own power—is there the possibility of improving your situation or creating a different story. If you see yourself as a passive character acted upon by (and then reacting to) external forces you neither understand nor control, you then become a helpless victim.

Along with this idea of self-agency comes another important idea. What is, *is*. While you have considerable power to change *what is*—if you learn how to harness it—there are limits to what you can do. Your real power comes, once you reach these limits, from how you *respond* to what is, not from misguided attempts to *control* it. How things are for you is to a great extent the product of how you *feel* about what's happening—and how you *feel* is the result of the *meaning* you've placed on what's happening. If you are living with conscious awareness, you will be happy and peaceful *because the meaning you have consciously given to what is happening is one that creates happiness and inner peace*.

Here is an interesting exercise to help you become more aware of how you assign meaning. Whenever you feel unhappy or distressed, ask yourself what meaning you've placed on what seems to be causing your suffering. Consider what other meanings you could give this situation that *would* allow you to be happy. Notice how attached you are to interpretations that cause you suffering. If you find that you're unwilling to let negative interpretations go in favor of those

PERSONAL EXPERIENCE

Yesterday was like most days, with frustrations coming from my husband's and my business, physical ills, etc. I felt confused. I walked into my husband's office with tears welling in my eyes and stuttered out, "I feel so disgusted!" This wasn't the right word to describe my feelings but it was all I could say. As I finished saying this, I decided the whole scene didn't feel right and remembered to take a mental step backwards. As I did, in a fleeting moment I heard, "there is no advantage to this." I immediately stopped the drama.

A little later on we left to run some errands, and while in the car I started to laugh because I realized that all day I had been trying very hard to get depressed as each thing happened which normally made me depressed, but I only felt confusion and some sort of odd feeling of "so what." Then I tried the "I'm really upset," teary number and that didn't work either. The more I thought about it the funnier it became. I also realized this drama was intended to get me sympathy and hopefully get someone else involved to solve the problem. And when they didn't, man, they were in trouble with me. Good grief!

At the moment I'm still feeling confused since my usual way of reacting no longer makes sense, and this way of behaving is totally foreign to me. I've decided to focus on what makes me feel good and "so what" to the rest!

The really far-out additional happening is going on with my husband. Our marriage had deteriorated into "two ships passing in the night." He is changing and having cognitions, and he only did about two weeks of the tapes and nothing in the last five weeks or so. I imagine my perceptions and cognitions have had an effect on him in some way. We are communicating!

—Gratefully, Carol O.

that create happiness and peace, then realize that this is your choice. The meanings you give to things have consequences, so choose wisely. And certainly don't just be an automatic response mechanism, mechanically and unconsciously assigning meanings you did not choose onto people, things, or situations and then experiencing consequences you do not want.

Your new meaning, the one leading to happiness, is no more real or intrinsic to the situation than the first meaning that led to suffering. This is because nothing has any *intrinsic* meaning. But if you are going to place a meaning on what is happening, which meaning would you want, the *happiness* meaning, or the *unhappiness* meaning? It is your choice, though most people don't realize it *is* a choice. This whole discussion, and the idea that you could really *choose* to be happy and peaceful, may sound utopian to you. Becoming conscious enough to notice when you're suffering, to notice what meaning you've placed on a situation, and to consciously change that meaning, doesn't come easily. Usually only those who have spent many years meditating or pursuing some other arduous spiritual practice gain this degree of conscious awareness. One of the central benefits of the Centerpointe program is that it creates this kind of awareness, and does so relatively quickly. Using Holosync® creates the ability to view things from a higher spot on the mountain, one allowing you to consciously make new and more resourceful choices.

Your Inner Map of Reality

ⓖ

I want to make these ideas a little more concrete by expanding on my earlier metaphor of an inner map. We all create maps of reality as we grow up. These templates allow us to instantly process and categorize a steady stream of information that would be overwhelming if we didn't have some way of understanding it quickly. Without our inner maps, we would have to figure out how to open a door each time we came to one, or relearn how to socialize every time we met a new person. These are simple examples. Your map of reality also contains and organizes countless beliefs, values, generalizations, decisions, and other concepts that pertain to how you see yourself in relation to the rest of the world.

Your internal map of reality is a blueprint your mind uses to create your life. Just because your inner map is incredibly useful to you, however, doesn't mean that it's the best one you could have, or that you're fated to live the rest of your life with the one you have now. As I've said, some inner maps are built around pain and insecurity and desperate attempts to remain safe by avoiding change, following the rules, and other non-resourceful strategies. These maps keep their owners and operators stuck in patterns that create suffer-

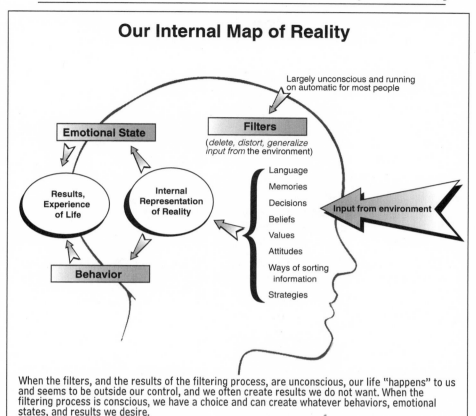

Our Internal Map of Reality

Largely unconscious and running on automatic for most people

Emotional State

Filters

(*delete, distort, generalize* input from the environment)

Results, Experience of Life

Internal Representation of Reality

Language

Memories

Decisions

Beliefs

Values

Attitudes

Ways of sorting information

Strategies

Input from environment

Behavior

When the filters, and the results of the filtering process, are unconscious, our life "happens" to us and seems to be outside our control, and we often create results we do not want. When the filtering process is conscious, we have a choice and can create whatever behaviors, emotional states, and results we desire.

ing. A person who learned early in life that the world is a scary place builds a map whose central purpose is to keep him safe. He believes he must do this in order to survive. This might be such a strong imperative that all of reality is seen through this lens, even though the actual danger was left behind years ago. Such a map would have big areas of darkness with black clouds and monsters and burning pits. You would think such a map would be discarded as soon as possible, but, strangely, we can become most attached to the issues that frighten us the most.

What helps us redraw our maps is remembering that we cannot drive on those little lines on the road map, and you can't go camping on those little triangles representing mountains. *The map is not the territory; it just represents the territory.* In just the same way, the internal map we create is not reality, but rather, a representation of reality. The map is not who you are; it's just the tool you're using at this time to conceptualize who you are.

This is good news. It means that you don't have to be stuck in fear and anger, or any other kind of suffering. You can change your map. And if your inner map begins to fall apart (as it might, for instance, as a result of the powerful push it gets from the Centerpointe program), that doesn't mean that *you're* falling apart. It just

Centerpointe Insight—Dealing With Worry

How to deal with worries can be expressed in a simple three-step formula, adapted from *How to Stop Worrying and Start Living* by Dale Carnegie:

1.   Analyze the situation and figure out what is the worst thing that can happen. Usually the worst that can happen, once we analyze it, though it may be bad, is not as bad as what we imagined before we really quantified it.

2.   Next, reconcile yourself to accepting the worst. You'll realize the world will not end if the worst happens. You'll muddle through somehow, as you've always done. At this point, you might think of other bad things that have happened in your life and how they usually did not turn out to be anywhere near as bad as you had originally thought they would be. In fact, many (if not most) of them ultimately turned out to be blessings in disguise, often being important turning points leading to something much better.

3.   Devote your time and energy to doing what can be done to improve on the worst-case scenario you envisioned in Step 2. With your mind now clearer, you'll be more effective in changing the situation.

Let's imagine the worst of the worst: let's say you learn you have a fatal disease. You imagine the worst: I may die. You reconcile yourself to the fact that this *will* happen. It eventually happens to us all, and there is no getting around it. The doctors are probably right. If I must die, then I must. Then get busy doing whatever you can, both to keep the doctors from being right and, also, to get the most out of whatever remaining life you have.

Have you ever known someone who was dying, knew they were dying, and had reconciled themselves to the fact? I have. Such a person radiates peace. Once you reconcile yourself to the worst that can happen, nothing can harm you. Then you can do whatever is possible to create a better outcome.

means that your understanding of who you are and what your relationship is to the rest of the world is inadequate for dealing with your environment and is about to expand.

When you begin to do deep transformational work, your internal map of reality will fall apart and re-form many times. Your map keeps changing as it becomes more resourceful and less dysfunctional. With some experience, you will be able to recognize these times of change, and at these times you have a choice. You can try to save the old map by resisting the process, or you can have faith that the process will yield a new map that will serve you better. If you let the change happen without resistance, the process is not only painless, it is joyful—even euphoric.

Because most people think their map of reality, their conceptual model of who they are and how they relate to the rest of the world, *is* who they are, they vigorously resist when that map begins to fall apart. To them, it feels as if *they* are falling apart; remember, however, *the map is not the territory*, and you are not your concept of who you are. You can learn to greet such transformations with this response: "Great! My old map of reality, which has a number of deficiencies that are causing me all kinds of suffering, is falling apart. That means I'll soon have a new map that works much better and allows me to be happier and more peaceful inside and deal more easily with whatever happens." Then you just stand aside and know that you'll soon be able to find your way to the "better neighborhood" that once seemed beyond your reach. Since you're not the map, it's no big deal if it falls apart; in fact, it's a big improvement!

Once most of the old emotional baggage, rules, and non-resourceful ways of responding are handled, a new kind of expansion of the map begins. All kinds of connections begin to fill in blank parts of the map, linking everything in the universe to every other thing—connections you never thought existed and never saw before. Now you see the universe as one big organism, one that you are a part of and an expression of. Since nothing is really outside you, your fear, anxiety, and stress dissolve; because if it's all you, there is nowhere to go, nothing to get, nothing to fear.

I can say with certainty that the further you go in the Centerpointe program, the more complex and realistic your map of reality will become and the more you'll feel at one with your environment. My advice is to make your inner map one of peace, happiness, and contentment, because the reality expressed in your map is what you'll experience as your life. But as I've said, it's your choice. Right now, chances are that most of your map of reality was created for you by outside forces and now simply runs automatically, creating an experience of life that seems like it is happening *to* you as a result of outside forces beyond your control. If that is the life you want, super. If not, you might want to find a way to consciously create the map you *do* want—and, as a result, the life you want.

The Reactor

Conscious living means becoming intentional rather than reactive. In our culture we are conditioned to react quickly to an ever-changing environment. You have to think fast and act fast to survive and prosper. "He who hesitates is lost." So you make deci-sions on the fly as you cruise through your hectic day. Sometimes it is essential to do this, trusting your intuition and your reflexes. If you suddenly notice that a fire has broken out in your home, you must act quickly to get to safety. There won't be time to sit and think things through. The ability to act quickly can save your life.

There is certainly a part of you that is absolutely present and automatic in any crisis. It is the part of you that reacts instantly. It's there to help you in time of danger, and it also helps you to be in the mo-

> **PERSONAL EXPERIENCE**
>
> I started meditating with Holosync about 3 years ago. I was very stressed-out, a single parent raising three children, one of whom is handicapped. I started meditating because I was stressed-out and I wanted change in my life. I was in an abusive relationship with a man who I couldn't muster up the emotional strength to leave. I hated that he controlled me and I hated myself for allowing it. Well, my life changed within a year. I met a wonderful man, fell in love and married him. My life is completely different now. I quit my casino job and am now a full time student. I had always wanted to go back to college but couldn't afford to quit my job.
>
> What I didn't realize was that if I hadn't used Holosync I wouldn't have made these changes in my life. I have been meditating for all this time and waiting for something BIG to happen and I finally realized that my new life is what happened! These changes happened over a period of one year, but I didn't SEE it as ME making this happen! I cannot believe this JUST hit me now!
>
> —AnnaMarie (from an e-mail)

Centerpointe Insight—Accepting What Is

When something happens that I don't like, first I generally do everything I can to change it. Sometimes I succeed, sometimes I don't. But often, "what is" wins, and I spend some time (hopefully, just a short moment) feeling at least mildly lousy about it. Then I realize what I'm doing (creating suffering), and I just decide to stop it and let it be okay. Then I feel great again, instantly.

Very occasionally, I feel lousy about something for as long as several hours, though it's usually much less. And I know I'm doing this because (for whatever weird reason), I *choose* to. Before I worked with Holosync, however, I could feel bad for months, years, or even decades about something over which I had no control. In fact, I was an expert in feeling bad. How I felt was not a choice because I didn't even know I *had* a choice. Now, as soon as I sense that old, bad feeling coming on, I remind myself that I'm creating whatever is happening. Then, I just let it go, right in that moment. It's actually easy for me to do now.

Suffering is voluntary for me now, and though I admit I occasionally still choose to suffer—sometimes it feels good to whine and complain for a little while—I can drop it anytime I want to. And as time goes on, I've become more and more bored with being upset about anything, and as that happens, those times become fewer and less frequent. This is the kind of conscious awareness and ability to choose that the Centerpointe program creates in those who use it.

ment, available for whatever is happening to you. Your beliefs, decisions, opinions, and emotional state are all shaped largely by the part of you that I call the *Reactor*.

But when it comes to your emotions, attitudes, and beliefs, living as the Reactor has its down side. As a reactor you can perpetually be in a state of fight or flight, or the captive of your passions. Reactors have triggers in their lives that activate their fear and anger. Something happens, and without thinking, they lash out.

It is as if we have a big toggle switch inside of us that some unknown person sometimes flips to the on position. Afterward we are horrified to see that, without meaning to, we have said something awful to our children, or have overreacted to a minor frustration and compromised our reputation as a levelheaded, trustworthy adult. Sometimes we are privately shaken by our own emotional reaction to something very ordinary. After the storm is over, we think about it in

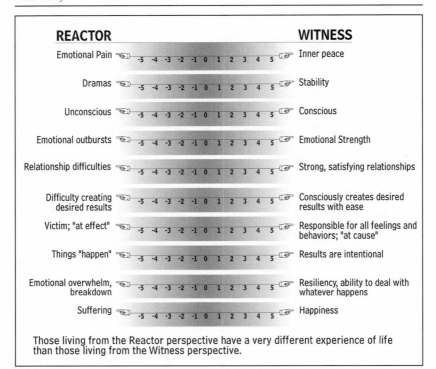

REACTOR		WITNESS
Emotional Pain	-5 -4 -3 -2 -1 0 1 2 3 4 5	Inner peace
Dramas	-5 -4 -3 -2 -1 0 1 2 3 4 5	Stability
Unconscious	-5 -4 -3 -2 -1 0 1 2 3 4 5	Conscious
Emotional outbursts	-5 -4 -3 -2 -1 0 1 2 3 4 5	Emotional Strength
Relationship difficulties	-5 -4 -3 -2 -1 0 1 2 3 4 5	Strong, satisfying relationships
Difficulty creating desired results	-5 -4 -3 -2 -1 0 1 2 3 4 5	Consciously creates desired results with ease
Victim; "at effect"	-5 -4 -3 -2 -1 0 1 2 3 4 5	Responsible for all feelings and behaviors; "at cause"
Things "happen"	-5 -4 -3 -2 -1 0 1 2 3 4 5	Results are intentional
Emotional overwhelm, breakdown	-5 -4 -3 -2 -1 0 1 2 3 4 5	Resiliency, ability to deal with whatever happens
Suffering	-5 -4 -3 -2 -1 0 1 2 3 4 5	Happiness

Those living from the Reactor perspective have a very different experience of life than those living from the Witness perspective.

a more calm and collected way and wish we'd reacted differently.

Perhaps that unknown person flipping the switch is our unconscious self. What we see in those moments of blind reaction is the power of the unconscious as it attempts to protect us from injuries that feel very much like ones we have suffered in the past. There are reasons we react the way we do, even if we don't know what they are. But remember, these reactions result from the meaning we've placed on a given situation, a meaning we probably did not choose or even know we could choose.

When we live in an unconscious way, present circumstances activate old wounds if the stimuli at all resembles past insults and injuries. Events can take us over, and we are at effect rather than at cause. We can damage our relationships with others and sabotage our efforts to succeed and thrive. Without intending to, we perpetuate destructive, dysfunctional cycles of behavior and belief. Unfortunately, it takes very little reinforcement for reactive behavior to become habitual.

Finding the Witness

At the other end of the spectrum from your Reactor is your *Witness*. I describe the Witness as the part of you that observes what is happening, even as it happens. When you observe in this way, you feel as if you are standing outside yourself and observing how you're feeling, what you are doing, and how you're interacting with your environment. The Reactor is the agent of knee-jerk responses, but the Witness just watches. From your Reactor's unconscious perspec-

---

Games You Can Play—Standing Aside from Your Pain

Several years ago, in the infancy of the Centerpointe program, a woman in the program called me in an extremely agitated state. "I'm freaking out!" she said. "I feel like I'm coming apart at the seams! Help!" She really was freaked out—as freaked out as a person can be and still communicate with someone else.

I told her to go lie down on her bed and very carefully notice the feelings that were happening in her body, to be very curious about every sensation, and then call me back and give me a report. Twenty minutes later she called to tell me that (darn it) she couldn't really give me much of a report because the whole feeling had disappeared as soon as she adopted that point of view of the curious watcher. All she felt then was a kind of euphoria, as if something had shifted for her!

---

tive, things look either good or bad, depending on the meaning you place on them. From your Witness's perspective, everything looks neutral and interesting, so the Witness just watches with curiosity, without evaluating.

The Witness part of you knows all along that life is just a game, and that you're making it up as you go along. To be really conscious, you must learn to come at life from the Witness perspective. There really is no other way. One way to do this is to consider yourself an actor in a play who consciously chooses the meaning of the unfolding story line. In this actor role, you're both author and Witness to what is happening.

For the conscious person, being the Witness is like turning on a searchlight that sweeps its beam over everything—illuminating and clarifying the complexities and the dark corners. Having the wider and clearer view, you can stand back a little and observe the passing scene. Instead of being involved in all the drama, you merely watch, monitoring whatever happens, like an omnipotent observer. As the Witness, while you're letting whatever happens be okay, you're also noting the things you want to do differently. Once you have the awareness to see the vicious cycles that were once hidden from you, you can learn new ways of functioning outside them. In fact, since it is impossible to continue to create suffering *consciously*, once you are *conscious,* these old ways of being are automatically replaced by new, resourceful ways of being. Being the Witness is so incredibly simple, yet it has tremendous power. But how do you do it?

Step back the next time you're feeling any kind of discomfort and say to yourself, "There I am, feeling angry (or whatever)." And then just notice yourself being in that emotion. Notice where you feel it in your body. Notice whether it stays in one place or moves around, and whether it stays the same or changes. Get out of wanting

Games You Can Play—
Being Hamlet versus Playing Hamlet

In *Hamlet* everyone suffers, and Hamlet, along with most of the other characters in the play, dies in the end. But we, the audience, are outside the play and understand that what is happening is not real, despite our very real emotions as we react to the characters and action. In like manner, the actors themselves know at all times that what is happening is not real.

Once you know you're dealing with a *map* of reality, you're like the actor who's playing Hamlet. Because he knows it's just a play, he can enjoy himself, despite the fact that everyone dies in the end. If the actor thinks he *is* Hamlet, however, he's going to be pretty miserable, considering what's going to happen. Learn to act the role of Hamlet, not *be* Hamlet. As long as you understand that you're an actor in a drama, life is fun and suffering falls away.

You can close the door to things from your past that may still upset you. You can say to yourself, "This has already happened; that scene is over, and it's not happening now. I've suffered and worried enough already, and after all, it's just a play, so I'm going to close the door on this and let it go."

the feeling to go away, and get into being genuinely curious about whatever is happening. Notice how difficult it is to stay stuck in your suffering if a part of you is watching. If you're curious and watching, it also becomes harder and harder to resist the flow of change. Curiosity is on the opposite side of the fence from resistance, and without resistance there is no suffering. So the antidote to resistance is simple: just watch. Whenever you notice discomfort, you know you're resisting, and that becomes a signal to—just watch.

Centerpointe Insight—Meditation and the Inner Witness

Meditation is, in part, a process of locating the inner Witness, that aspect of our awareness which is capable of stepping into that moment between the arising of a powerful feeling and our identification with it. As our awareness becomes focused as the Witness, we begin to see elements of our emotional and mental functioning at work. We witness a series of processes and realize they've done more than just create an impact in the moment, they've also determined much of how we've lived our lives to that point.

All well-developed spiritual traditions teach about the Witness, though often in different words. Some traditions speak of detachment, others of being in the world but not "of it." For centuries meditators and spiritual seekers have sought to tap into the Witness, to learn from it, to inhabit it as a means of gaining insight and deeper information about themselves and the world around them. Of course, when someone sets out to do this, the first thing they notice is just how reactive they really are. In fact, the real answer to the question of what to do when you're resisting (whether the resistance is conscious or unconscious) is to just watch with that witnessing part of yourself. Stop fighting with yourself and just *notice* what's happening. Become truly curious about it and just watch. Distress and discomfort fall away when you do this, almost as if by magic. *If resistance is the poison that creates suffering, being the Witness is the antidote that creates peace and happiness.*

Every day we communicate with dozens of people who are using the Centerpointe program, and some of them are having a hard time. Sometimes these people are angry, depressed, fearful, anxious, confused, or are creating any number of other responses to the events of their lives. One of the principal pieces of advice we give these people is to watch what's happening.

PERSONAL EXPERIENCE

In 1991, I was employed as a music teacher in an inner city Toronto school. Over time, I noticed that I became increasingly fatigued and had difficulty concentrating. I just chalked this up to the stress of the job. Eventually it became bad enough that I had to leave my position and go on long term disability and stay with my elderly parents.

My doctor referred me to psychiatrists, who told me I was depressed and promptly started me on a regimen of antidepressants and tranquilizers. I began to experience panic attacks and was prescribed Xanax. This stuff turned me into a basket case, and I was hospitalized. While in the hospital, I was prescribed amphetamines and was discharged. Well, I didn't feel depressed but I was euphoric and at the same time, tragically, a long-term relationship ended.

Now, during this time, I was diagnosed with having multiple sclerosis but was continued on a combination of amphetamines and Valium! By this time, I had been on so many different drugs that I suffered a drug-induced psychosis. I was paranoid, suspicious and hostile. My contract with the school board was also officially terminated. It gets worse! After 3 months in the hospital I was discharged because they could do nothing for me.

For two whole years I stayed in bed and at night just wandered around the house unable to sleep. I could not stand to take showers or go outdoors. I was unable to read or watch TV. I am a classical guitarist and did not even take my instrument out of its case. Twice I overdosed in an attempt to sleep or at least feel better and twice I almost died. Unbelievable, but I swear it's the truth!

Eventually, my girlfriend, who miraculously always stood by me during these horrible years, took me to see an internist. He took one look at the long list of symptoms I had written and said, "I don't believe there is anything wrong with you. This is the profile of someone on drugs. Your only problem is drugs." At first, I didn't want to believe him. I was so sure there must be a drug out there that could help me. But, somehow through my drug induced stupor I asked myself, "What if he's right?"

I went home and quit everything cold turkey. Some of these drugs can stay in a person's system for up to two years. One day at an intersection, on my way to school, I failed to stop at a red light, was hit broadside, and my car was a total write-off. I was lucky. A split second difference and I would have been killed. Everything was chaos! Nothing made sense. How much can a person take?

The one thing that helped me survive was a skill that you, Bill, often emphasize, and that is "Watching!" Now, I hope no one else has to go through this particular adventure. Watching works and it is one positive thing that I brought with me through that experience. It is definitely helping me in the Centerpointe program.

In conclusion, (finally!) let me say that since I have started your program, I have experienced relief from many MS symptoms including better concentration, better memory, increased energy, better sleep and better health overall. I once again have a loving relationship with my family, am playing the guitar again, and am now engaged. And I will be starting school again in May. Life is once again worth living.

—Frederik (via email)

I know you'd be much more impressed if I could somehow make this more complex, more elegantly complicated, but what can I do? It's that simple. When you feel discomfort, instead of resisting, just watch.

I don't think most people could say what happens to their bodies when they are angry. They are too unconscious to notice. When you are curious, however, you stop being caught up in being angry, and the anger seems to disappear. You can't do this directly by saying, "Now I'm going to get rid of the anger." You really have to become curious. When you watch what happens when you suffer, the suffering goes away.

One of the most important things I've noticed over my seventeen years of working with Holosync is how relentlessly the program moves you from being unconscious to being more aware. The Witness becomes more and more prominent, easier to summon when needed, and soon becomes a constant companion. You begin to understand why you're having certain feelings, where these

A Story

A friend in the Centerpointe program sent this bit of verse to me. While I don't know its source, I do know that it says perfectly what I want to convey about adopting the role of the actor, Witness, or author who is able to give his heart to the game of life, knowing all the while that it is a great diversion and will eventually end.

> When the Macedonians deserted him,
> the noble King Dimitrios didn't behave
> —so it is said—
> at all like a King.
> He took off his golden robes,
> discarded his purple buskins,
> and quickly dressing himself
> in simple clothes, he slipped out—
> just like an actor who,
> the play over,
> changes his costume and goes away.

Adopt the posture of being the Witness, curious but detached. Doing so gives you choice, and this allows you to *choose happiness*, instead of waiting for it to come to you.

feelings come from, and what your options are for responding—or not responding—and how you can choose to create something better and happier. Because of this shift toward being more fully alive and awake, you can live a more purposeful and more intentional life. At a certain point it becomes very clear that you really can choose what to think and how to feel about what happens to you.

Expanding Your Awareness

I believe that living in this more conscious state is what people mean when they talk about expanded awareness. For some people this concept has the flavor of mysticism, and there's no doubt that some people do have mystical experiences as a result of meditation. But what I want to emphasize here is something simpler: *in daily life it's possible for us ordinary people to live consciously from moment to moment, and if we do so, we can't help but be happy and peaceful.*

Here are the elements we've identified that can help you live a life that is inner directed, constantly evolving, resilient in the face of external difficulties, and at peace:

- Realize that you are the creator of your own reality. You can make choices, if you will only exercise your ability to do so.
- Your interpretation of reality is based upon an inner map, most elements of which you did not choose. You have the power to change your map if you want to.
- You can redraw your inner map to be more authentic, more resourceful, and less limiting.
- To the extent that you're creating your map consciously rather than unconsciously, each new map will serve you better than the last.
- You can learn to live consciously by calling on that part of you who is the Witness.
- The more often you are the Witness, the less often you will be the Reactor.
- Involvement in the Centerpointe program will facilitate and accelerate this process of personal evolution into the conscious living that is the hallmark of happy, peaceful people.
- Now that you understand this process, you can welcome (and watch) change, rather than resisting it.

Q & A—
How Can You Become More Conscious?

Part of what you can do to hasten the process of becoming more conscious is make a catalog of all the non-resourceful and painful things you believe about yourself, about other people, and about the world. Many of these beliefs may be outside of awareness and impossible to verbalize, but they'll tend to come out in your self-talk—especially when you're feeling bad about yourself. By watching that self-talk, you can uncover these beliefs. When something bad happens, you may, for instance, say to yourself, "No one cares what happens to me." This represents a belief about yourself. As I've said, your beliefs tend to create your life and your circumstances. No wonder you're angry, anxious, fearful, or depressed! Change them and the circum- stances of your life will change, too. The problem is that it's not easy, because a part of us wants to hang on to these old beliefs because they *seem* to be true, and what's more, we often associate them with our safety.

Once you've uncovered these beliefs (an on-going process), you must convince yourself that they're not worth having, even though, as a result of your upbringing and history, they seem to be true. In fact, whether they're true or false is not really the most useful distinction to make about them, especially since these beliefs are actually *meanings* that have been superimposed on a neutral reality. The most helpful distinction to make about these beliefs is whether or not they're *resourceful*, whether they contribute to happiness and peace, or to suffering and unhappi- ness. Then, from a more conscious perspective, knowing that you're placing a new meaning on what is, you can decide what a more resourceful belief would be in each case, and then begin inculcating your mind with that belief. This time, however, you know that you're consciously choosing this new belief not because it's true, but simply because it's more resourceful and will lead to greater peace and happiness.

Is this difficult to do? It can be, but as you move through the Centerpointe program and become increasingly conscious and aware, it becomes easier and easier. In fact, as you master the ability to be the Witness, it begins to happen automatically.

As you practice conscious awareness and continue using the Centerpointe program, expanded awareness grows even greater, until it begins to include an increased sense of connection with the rest of the universe. But it begins with the simple ability to reserve a small part of you to just watch yourself, and whatever is happening, with detachment and curiosity. As you master this ability, a whole new world will open up for you—one that is happy and peaceful, and in which you somehow intuitively know just what to do and how to be in every situation. From that perspective, life is truly wonderful.

Games You Can Play—Remind Yourself of the Witness

Though your daily use of Holosync will cause the development of a kind of super-awareness no matter what other growth activities you engage in, there are other things you can do to facilitate its development. First of all, you can remind yourself several times a day to watch what is happening. Just spend a few minutes every time it occurs to you to just sit back and notice what's going on. How does your body feel? What is your mind doing? What is going on around you? Does any of this change as you watch?

Soon you'll find yourself, even when caught up in the midst of activity, with a little part of you noticing everything that is going on. It's a new perspective, one that isn't caught up in whatever is going on.

This is the beginning of expanded awareness.

I SAID TO MY SOUL, BE STILL AND WAIT WITHOUT HOPE
FOR HOPE WOULD BE HOPE FOR THE WRONG THING; WAIT WITHOUT LOVE
FOR LOVE WOULD BE LOVE OF THE WRONG THING; THERE IS YET FAITH BUT
THE FAITH AND THE LOVE AND THE HOPE ARE ALL IN THE WAITING.
WAIT WITHOUT THOUGHT, FOR YOU ARE NOT READY FOR THOUGHT;
SO THE DARKNESS SHALL BE THE LIGHT, AND THE STILLNESS THE DANCING.

—T. S. ELIOT, FOUR QUARTETS

CHAPTER 7

Your Threshold to the Future

Those beautiful lines from T. S. Eliot contain a key to understanding the process of evolutionary growth we have been discussing: that the most amazing things happen when we are able to be still and wait. Even more, if we can wait in a spirit of openness and receptivity, without attachment to the demands of the ego, we can expect the transformation of darkness into light and stillness into dancing. Sometimes these transformations are life-changing and revolutionary, but more often than not, they are incremental and evolutionary.

We call those moments of revelation or transformation *felt shifts*, a term first used, as far as I know, by Eugene Gendlin in his book *Focusing* (New York: Bantam Books, 1981.) Felt shifts are quantum leaps, in which an old way of seeing or experiencing yourself, other people, or the world, changes in a fundamental way. From the ashes of the old, something new arises. Inside yourself, you can tell that something has fallen into place or taken shape in a new way.

History is filled with accounts of felt shifts that had momentous consequences beyond the life of the individual. Examples that changed history include the conversion of St. Paul on the road to Damascus, Emperor Constantine's vision of the cross by which he was to conquer, Joan of Arc's voices that led her to mount a campaign against the English, and the Buddha's enlightenment beneath the Bodhi tree. To find examples that are no less momentous, but confined to the personal experience of the individual, we must move our gaze to private diaries and confessions.

A friend of mine, a history professor, recalls experiencing a felt shift while he was present as Martin Luther King, Jr. delivered his "I Have a Dream" speech in 1963. "Dr. King was talking about a vision he had of what the future of America could be. And as he was talking I closed my eyes and saw it. The whole thing. Peace. The end of racial division. And I saw that the vision Dr. King was talking about could never come true unless I changed. So I released my fears about changing my life and let it all go. My life changed forever that day at the Lincoln Memorial."

Felt Shifts and Growth

It may be human to yearn for the all-encompassing "on-the-road-to-Damascus" kind of shift that transforms us in an instant and sets us on fire with energy and passion. But we must also develop a sensitivity to lesser shifts. For most people, most of the time, change happens as an accumulation of smaller shifts over time. These shifts may even happen out of our awareness and not be discovered for some time after they've occurred.

As many of us know, felt shifts rarely happen when we're busy looking for them. Having such an experience is like having a butterfly land on your shoulder. You can't force it to happen, but when it does, it brings with it a sense of magic. We awaken in some way, and have direct contact with something far deeper and greater than we previously imagined existed. At Centerpointe, we try to focus on the bigger picture of growth instead of on these heart-stopping moments of metamorphosis. If they happen, great! If not, don't worry about it. The final result is the same. Like the watched pot that never boils, transformation doesn't necessarily reward anxious watchfulness. It does, however, reward daily practice. Whether the changes happen for you in big leaps or small ones, they will not happen at all if you are not using the program regularly. And they will not happen if you are unwilling to face the unresolved residue of your past, or if you block your own path on the inward journey by holding fast to what is familiar.

If there is one thing I have learned in my many years of administrating the Centerpointe program, it is that in order to change, we must be willing to give up the old way of being. If the way we see things does not change, if we hang on to the old, we will continue to get the same results. Those who experience big, life-changing shifts must be willing to try on a new way of seeing themselves, other people, and the world. The irony of personal growth is that people cling tightly to old ways of being, despite the fact that those ways of being are creating disastrous results in their lives. Luckily, daily meditation with Holosync® lessens this fear of change and moves us toward that place where we can get out of the way and allow beneficial changes to happen.

But even if you *do* get out of your own way and allow growth and change to happen, you still come back to a world that hasn't changed. All the things you've always found disturbing are still there, and you are still living in a world where people are busy acting out of dysfunction and creating suffering for themselves and others.

So, then, why do things feel so different? Because *you have developed a different perspective.* Your map of reality is new. You are looking at life through a new lens. Things are as they were before, except that you are experiencing them in a new way. Buddhists call this *developing compassion.* Instead of reacting to the bad in the world, or in yourself, with anger or sadness or despair, and experiencing suffering because of it, you now accept *what is* and feel that everything is somehow happening just as it should. You feel compassion for suffering but are no longer caught up in it. But this does not mean you don't care. This little bit of positive distance allows you to become more effective in taking action, because you are not as reactive or fearful as you used to be.

Your threshold for stress is much, much higher, so events around you cannot push you into reaction. You are much more accepting of your own human failings as well as those of others. You are seeing life from a higher spot on the mountain, and it really does look much different. You are no longer helplessly caught in it all. You are a player in a play and you relish your part in the unfolding story. Most of all, you are no longer in a hurry, because you are content in each moment even if you aren't "there" yet (wherever that is for you). The inner journey is full of interest, full of rewards. You can enjoy yourself as you are right now, confident that your evolution is progressing in exactly the right way. You are doing what you need to do, and you have faith in the rest.

When I started Centerpointe back in 1989, my believe was that all a person needed to do was meditate daily with Holosync, and everything would happen on its own. And, in a sense, this is true. Listening to Holosync every day does plow through the resistance and push you to change, even if there are occasional moments of discomfort.

But there is an even easier way, and I stumbled onto it as a result of the Centerpointe retreats we hold several times each year. In these retreats, about fifty Centerpointe participants gather from all over the world at a spa, hot springs, or retreat center for a week of intensive inner work. During this time, we meditate for several hours a day with some very powerful Holosync soundtracks, and I speak extensively about the program and how it works. In addition, my incredible retreat staff takes everyone through a number of experiential processes designed to help people understand the process of change on a very deep level and learn how to get out of the way and just let it happen.

Somehow, something magical happens at these retreats. People leave them changed in a fundamental way. Within a day or two, the participants feel closer to each other than they have ever felt to anyone, and though no one is forced to do so, people feel safe enough to share some of their deepest longings, fears, aspirations, and concerns with the group. All of this happens in an environment of total acceptance and love—in most cases the first time many of the participants have experienced such a feeling.

After several retreats, as I contemplated the amazing changes experienced by these people, I realized that at the retreats people learned some basic principles about how to live a life that is happy, peaceful, resourceful, and resilient. And though this information is found throughout the support material we sent to all program participants, I realized we were not doing as good a job as we could of teaching these principles to those who could not attend a retreat. This led to my formulating what I call my *Nine Principles for Happiness and Healing.*

Because I think these principles are so important, and because

I've seen such powerful positive change in people who master them, I want to end the book by describing them for you. Some of these principles I had heard about or read about in one form or another before my experience with Holosync, but then they were just bits of intellectual information. I did not understand them on an experiential level. As you use the program, you will probably have the same experience I had: intellectual recognition, followed later by a much more powerful inner knowing and an ability to really live the *Nine Principles*. This deeper understanding has made all the difference to me. Because the process of personal change resembles a spiral than a straight line, you may find yourself returning to the *Nine Principles* again and again as you revisit your own personal issues at deeper and deeper levels.

Finally, because I have mentioned several of these principles earlier in this book, presenting them serves as a summary of many of the important points you have been reading about.

The Nine Principles for Happiness and Healing

Understanding and practicing these principles is one of those easy-hard things in life—easy once you master them but seemingly impossible before you get them. If you can live your life by these principles, everything flows, suffering is minimal, and apparent problems melt away. As you set out to follow them, cut yourself some slack. Although they can be read and understood instantly, learning to live them will take some time. You'll probably find yourself stumbling over and over. Let that be okay. You'll go through several stages as you integrate each principle.

Stage One is Unconscious Incompetence, when you do not follow the principles and don't know you are not following them.

Stage Two is Conscious Incompetence. This is where you will be after reading this chapter. You are aware of the principles, but are not yet following them—but at least you know you aren't.

Stage Three is Conscious Competence, when you can follow the principles, but only when you're consciously making an effort.

Stage Four, Unconscious Competence, is when you have consciously followed the principle so consistently that it is second nature and no longer requires conscious attention. You are living them without thinking about it.

1. The Principle of Letting Whatever Happens Be Okay

The amount you suffer in life is directly related to how much you are resisting the fact that things are the way they are.

As I have said, whenever there is suffering or discomfort, there is resistance. There are no exceptions to this rule. *All* suffering, all discomfort, regardless of the appearance, is the result of resistance to something. Being addicted or attached to things being other than the way they are is a losing strategy. You will find that when your needs and attachments are changed to *preferences*, you can let go of your need for control over the uncontrollable. Then, when *what is* is not what you want it to be, you do not suffer over it. Other people and external events do not control your happiness and peace. You will escape suffering *only* to the degree you are willing and able to let whatever happens be okay. People who live by rules, shoulds, or have-to's tend to suffer quite often because no matter how hard these people work to protect their rules and see that others follow them, the rules are going to be violated sometimes. The more rules you have, and the more inflexible these rules are, the more often they will be violated, and the more often you will create suffering for yourself.

Letting whatever happens be okay does not mean you shouldn't be goal directed or that you can't work toward making your preferences into reality. It just means that when things are not the way you want, you do not have to suffer. You work toward the outcome you want, but are unattached to the results.

Neither does it mean you do not care about the suffering of others or the presence of oppression or evil in the world. It just means you do not suffer emotionally as a result. Your suffering is replaced by a deep compassion for all beings (including yourself). Because you are not caught up in suffering, but instead are moved by compassion, you somehow know exactly what to do and have the conscious awareness and presence of mind to act effectively and appropriately. You become *more* effective, and your attempts to bring about change are also much more effective because they are better focused and more appropriate.

The key, then, to handling challenging situations, thoughts, and feelings is not in resisting them, but in accepting their existence as completely as you can. Through acceptance you empower yourself to heal, transform, or release any unresolved mental or emotional material. Accept what happens to you; accept what you think and feel, even when it is uncomfortable to do so.

Alcoholics Anonymous beautifully expresses this principle in their "Serenity Prayer":

> *GOD, grant me the serenity to accept*
> *the things I cannot change,*
> *Courage to change the things I can,*
> *and the wisdom to know the difference.*
>
> —*Reinhold Neibuhr, 1926*

As I said earlier in this book, even though it looks as if the thing you resist creates the discomfort you feel, the fact is that all discomfort comes from your *resistance* to that thing. When you stop resisting, the discomfort stops. There may still be a sensation, and the sensation may be intense, but this intensity will not be negative unless you are resisting it. And perhaps more important, once you stop resisting, you will find that you are much more effective in creating any external change you may have a preference for (not an attachment to). During those times when you do sense your own resistance, however, learn to meet even this resistance with the same spirit of acceptance.

Remember the Witness from the previous chapter? One of the beauties of the Centerpointe program is that, as you progress, it becomes progressively easier to let whatever happens be okay. Why? Because the program develops in you a natural ability to be the Witness, and being the Witness is the antidote to the poison of resistance and the suffering it creates.

2. The Principle of Threshold

You have a personal threshold for what you can handle coming at you from your environment, based on your personal map of reality. All dysfunctional feelings and behaviors are really coping methods we use in an attempt to deal with being pushed over this threshold.

When your inner map isn't adequate to negotiate the challenges of your environment, you feel stressed and begin to use various coping mechanisms learned during childhood. These include anger, depression, anxiety, fear, substance abuse, overeating, sexual acting out, and possibly even more serious emotional problems such as personality disorders and even psychosis. These coping mechanisms can also take the form of behaviors generally considered to be healthy, such as exercising, talking with friends or counselors, isolating yourself, or burying yourself in work.

All dysfunctional feelings and behaviors are really mechanisms for dealing with the stress of being pushed past your personal threshold. The cure for dysfunctional feelings and behaviors, then, is to raise that threshold, which is what Holosync does. Dysfunctional feelings and behaviors are not caused by your environment or by other people, regardless of how it seems, and treating the symptoms (though sometimes necessary in the short term) is an overall dead-end. People with a high threshold for what they can handle remain happy, peaceful, and centered even when around difficult people or in difficult situations. Because raising your personal threshold for what happens treats the root cause, it offers the possibility for ending all dysfunction—and doing so permanently.

You now know that people who have been traumatized in some way or who have otherwise had significant negative emotional experiences have a lower thresholds than those who have not experienced trauma or whose trauma was less severe. You also know that, as a result, these people are more often caught in dysfunctional feelings and behaviors and the resultant suffering. The Centerpointe program is designed to raise your threshold until it is so high nothing can push you over it. As this happens, dysfunctional feelings and behaviors disappear.

The Nine Principles for Happiness and Healing

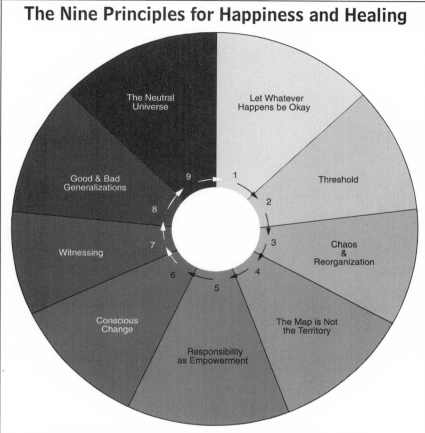

The Nine Principles are all facets of the same basic truth: That we each create our experience of life and can create the experience we want. We do this by first bringing into conscious awareness what was previously unconsciously running on automatic, and then making new decisions and new choices that better serve us and lead to the experience of life we wish to have.

3. The Principle of Chaos and Reorganization

Chaos is an essential part of the growth process, and should be welcomed rather than resisted. It represents the death of the old and the birth of the new.

Recall that the open systems theory of physicist Ilya Prigogine gives us a model for how complex systems, including human beings, grow and change. Simply put

- Each person has an upper limit to the amount of input they can handle (their personal threshold), and this limit is based on how much entropy, or chaos, the system can dissipate.

- If the system experiences too much input, the system cannot dissipate this chaos and it builds up inside the system.

- If this continues for long enough, the system will eventually reach a point where the chaos becomes so great that the system cannot hold itself together any longer. As a result, the system breaks down, ceasing to exist in the old way—but at the same moment, it instantaneously reorganizes itself at a higher, more complex level. This transformation is a true death and rebirth, a quantum leap to a whole new way of being.

- The main characteristic of this new system is that it can easily handle the input, the complexity, the intensity, that the old system could not handle. Because the new system has a new and greater resiliency, a greater plasticity, and a greater ability to flow with whatever is happening, what was once over-whelming is now easily dealt with.

We can be partners in this process by not reacting to the temporary chaos of change as though it were a problem. Our resistance to this chaos period is the source of all our suffering; stepping aside and watching the system reorganize at a higher level makes growth easy. Remember too, when we find ourselves in this interim period of chaos that always precedes positive change, we shouldn't conclude that we've regressed, or that the program isn't working. Even in advanced stages of the growth process, each new change will be preceded by chaos. When you're in the initial chaos state, remind yourself that this is the prelude to positive change. Feeling this chaos should be a signal to step back and watch the process with curiosity, which allows everything to happen more easily and with little or no suffering.

4. The Principle that The Map is Not the Territory

There is a tendency to protect our old map of reality when we go into the initial chaos stage of growth, because we mistakenly think we are the map.

Another way to say this is that we are more than our ideas and concepts of who we are. As I have said, we create an internal map of who we are and how we relate to the rest of the world while we are growing up. This map is useful as we travel through life because, just like a real map, it scales things down to a level of complexity we can more easily handle. However, as we get older and that map needs to change, we often try to hold onto the old map because we forget that it is just a tool we created. Instead, we mistake it for reality. Because it is largely unconscious and because we do not remember creating it, we think this internal concept of who we are *is* who we are. But the map is not the territory. It is just a symbolic picture, a convenient schematic, an approximate representation. We protect it because when it starts to fall apart we mistakenly think *we* are falling apart.

Trying to hold onto the old map creates suffering. Because suffering comes from trying to control the uncontrollable, it is better to open your clenched fist and let the old map go. Once you do this, you find you're relieved of the problems and limitations of the old blueprint and have a new ability to deal with what was previously stressful or overwhelming.

5. The Principle of Responsibility as Empowerment

You are responsible for every feeling or behavior you have.
You have either consciously chosen it, or you are unconsciously responding based on old, unconscious mental programming you did not choose.

Everyone who has been on a personal growth path for any length of time has been told that "you are the creator of your world," or "you are not a victim," or some variation thereof. Most would agree with these statements. However, in a real-life situation where something happens we don't like, many people—even those who have "been meditating 75 years" or "knew Werner Erhardt personally and helped design all his trainings" or who claim to have taken every personal growth training and read every self-help book on Earth (twice)—begin blaming something outside of themselves for what's happening.

Giving lip service to these principles is not going to help you. Intelligent and sophisticated sophistries to convince you and others that you are not responsible for what is happening in your life are not going to help, either. Why? Because until you realize that you create your experience of your world, including all happiness and all suffering, you will be at the effect end of the cause-and-effect process. You, and your experience of life, will be controlled by, and be at the whim of, whatever is happening around you. Your only chance for happiness will be to find perfect circumstances and to find a way to keep them that way—and you know how likely that is.

As I have said, this is not the same as saying you are *to blame* for every feeling or behavior you have. Taking personal responsibility is not about blame, but rather about personal power. If someone or something outside of you is the cause of how you feel or behave, you are powerless—a victim. If you, or at least your unconscious processes, are *at cause*, you have power to do something to change the situation to one that is happier and more peaceful. Things outside of you may be *stimuli* for you, but how you respond comes from you, either consciously or unconsciously.

You can live in a world where other people or events cause you to feel the way you feel, but there is a price: you will feel bad a great deal of the time. There is, however, another choice. You can choose to take responsibility for every feeling and every behavior. Doing so puts you at the cause end of the cause-and-effect process, where you can choose how you feel and how you behave.

Over the past several decades, our culture has gravitated toward the popularization of victimhood. The view is that no one is responsible for anything that happens to them. Smokers are not responsible for getting lung cancer; shooters of guns are not responsible for firing them. These days, burglars even sue homeowners for injuries they received while breaking into a house. Criminals are not responsible for crimes they commit because they had unhappy childhoods, or were under the influence of drugs. Battering husbands (or wives) are not responsible for beating their spouses because the other made them angry, or did such and such to them. These are the more extreme cases, but you can, I'm sure, fill in the details from your own life, if you're honest.

At the same time, it's so easy to say "I can't do _____. I have _____ (traumatic stress disorder, a cold, Attention Deficit Disorder, alcoholism, no money, don't read well, my father was distant, my mother was smothering, I grew up in the inner city, I grew up in the country, I'm black, I'm white, I'm tall, I'm short, and on and on)." In this popularization of victimhood, there is an underlying presupposition that it is somehow easier to be a victim, and that taking responsibility would be onerous, difficult, a struggle, too much work.

I would like to put forward the idea that it is being a victim that is onerous, difficult, a struggle, and too much work. Being responsible for everything that happens, and for every feeling and behavior, is the *easy* way to live. It is the way to happiness, inner peace, and a productive life. It is a way to end all the dramas in your life.

6. The Principle of Conscious Change

It is not possible to continue a feeling, behavior, or way of being that does not serve you, or in some way is not resourceful for you, and also do so consciously. Become conscious and what does not serve you falls away.

Using Centerpointe program soundtracks with Holosync technology will, over time, allow you to develop conscious awareness of how you operate, in both your internal and external worlds. As you become more aware of how you operate, your non-resourceful feelings and behaviors will automatically fall away and be replaced by healthier approaches that bring happiness and peace to your life. What does it mean to be conscious? This term is almost a cliche in personal growth, but few people understand what it really means, and even fewer are able to actually *do* it.

Being conscious means not operating as an automatic response mechanism. It mean being able to observe what is happening, on all levels simultaneously, at every moment, and to choose an emotional, mental, or behavioral response based on what is the most resourceful choice in that moment. Ultimately, it means doing all of this automatically, without conscious thought (there is a seeming contradiction: being conscious, but doing it automatically!). When you are consciously aware, a part of you learns to process all the possibilities in a split second and respond in just the right way—not with a preset rule or response (which is what I mean by being an automatic response mechanism), but with a choice that is optimum for the situation.

Most people, as I have said, are running on automatic. They have rules or set procedures for what to think, what to feel, and what to do in various situations—rules or procedures they learned when they were too young to know any better. And, these responses happen automatically, as Pavlov's dog salivated when it heard the dinner bell. Some of these responses were learned through physical or emotional pain and are deeply imbedded. Others are just things we accepted because our parents or teachers told us they were true when we were very young and these people seemed infallible to us.

Many of these rules and procedures are attempts to deal with our anxiety, or what I often refer to as overwhelm. We feel anxious so we withdraw, get angry, have a cigarette, eat, exercise, act silly, have a drink, talk too much, space out, have sex, tense up, buy something, watch TV, cry—or one of thousands of other behaviors or feelings. We don't choose them because they seemed to be the most resourceful action at the time. We just do them, automatically. Usually they're anything but resourceful. Often, they lead to drama, suffering, problems, and sadness.

People who have lived much of their lives without conscious awareness don't know they are doing it, and you may not believe me when I tell you that you are probably doing it, too—and doing it most, if not all, of the time. It takes becoming more conscious to look back and see just how unconscious your life was before your awakening. When Centerpointe support materials describe the idea of being the Witness, when we say "just watch with curiosity," we are trying to get you to begin the process of becoming more conscious.

Here, though, is the big benefit of being more conscious: It is impossible to do something that is not good for you, or is in some way non-resourceful (destructive) to you, and do it consciously. You can do something destructive to yourself (expressed through feelings, beliefs, values, behaviors, etc.) over and over as long as you do so unconsciously (in other words, without continuous conscious awareness). But begin to do the non-resourceful feeling, behavior, belief, value, etc. *consciously* and it will begin to fall away. You just can't consciously do something that isn't good for you.

The trick, of course, is to remain conscious, which is one of those things, like riding your bike or tying your shoe, that seems difficult until you get it—and then seems so easy you wonder why you ever thought it was hard. For this reason, as you unravel the mystery of what it means to be conscious in your own life, don't let yourself be discouraged. Keep going, keep trying, and keep watching, because at some point you'll be doing it, and it will all make sense.

I have already enumerated the many ways of going unconscious so as not to deal with what we're feeling or how we're behaving: overeating, drugs and alcohol, anger, and so on. To become conscious, you must (a) identify your favorite ways of going unconscious, (b) be vigilant in noticing them, and (c) be committed to gradually learning to be the Witness instead of allowing yourself to operate on automatic. This means developing the ability to be the Witness to what is happening, developing that part of you that can stand aside and notice what you are doing, feeling, or thinking—*as you do it*, watching without judgement or comment, just watching with curiosity, like a scientist.

7. The Principle of Witnessing

The ability to step aside and watch yourself as you feel and act is an acquired skill that takes time and practice to develop. But doing so will profoundly change your life. This skill is the antidote to resistance, which means it is your primary tool to end suffering in your life.

I have mentioned that one of the main instructions we give people who are having a hard time with the program is to watch what's happening—to watch with curiosity. This is a deceptively simple instruction that nonetheless has tremendous power.

Step back the next time you're feeling any kind of discomfort and say to yourself, "There I am, feeling angry" (or whatever), and then just notice yourself being angry. Any feeling you have will be a sensation in your body, so just notice where in your body you feel it. Notice if it stays in one place or moves around, if it stays the same or changes. Be curious. You don't care what that feeling does. Remember the scientist I mentioned, the one who had been searching the Amazon jungle for 20 years for a certain butterfly. Be that scientist. Bring that level of curiosity to bear on whatever is happening to you in that moment.

Notice that you cannot be a stuck in your suffering if a part of you is watching. If you are curious and watching, you cannot resist, and if you don't resist, you don't suffer. Curiosity is on the opposite side of the fence from resistance. Once you are successfully watching, it becomes obvious that you could choose another response to whatever is happening—even when a moment before there seemed to be *no* choice.

As people go through the Centerpointe program, the Witness becomes more and more prominent, more and more easy to summon when needed, and soon becomes a constant companion. This is the beginning of what spiritual teachers call expanded awareness. From this point on, expanded awareness grows even greater, to eventually include a sense of connection with the entire universe. But it begins with the simple ability to reserve a small part of you that just watches yourself and whatever is happening with detachment and curiosity.

So if resistance is your middle name, as it was for me, please take very seriously this simple instruction to watch with curiosity. It takes some practice and willpower because the habit of resisting is deeply ingrained and very much an automatic response. But with practice it will become an effortless part of you and will help you move easily through any situation you encounter.

I have written here mostly about resistance as it occurs from time to time in people using the Centerpointe Program, but this principle applies to life outside the program as well. In *any* situation where you're uncomfortable, step aside and watch. All people who are happy and internally peaceful have mastered this principle of witnessing. You can do it, too.

8. The Principle of Good and Bad Generalizations

Since whatever you believe and focus on comes true in reality, you can create whatever life and whatever reality you want once you learn to consciously choose what you focus on.

By now, you know I believe that it is not necessary to live a life containing suffering, and that it is entirely possible to live a life of happiness and inner peace. You also know that, in my opinion, the way to do this is to cultivate the ability to let whatever happens be okay and to not resist *what is*.

Not resisting *what is* does not mean you cannot want to change *what is*, and the difference is one of attachment to the outcome. A person who is attached to the outcome suffers if he does not get the outcome he wants, whereas the happy, peaceful person *prefers* the outcome he wants but is not attached to it. If he gets a different outcome, he remains just as happy and peaceful as he was to begin with. His happiness comes from within, and does not depend on what goes on around him.

Many people, however, are not only unhappy as a result of what goes on around them, but also because of what goes on *inside*. At the same time, this inner unhappiness helps create outside conditions that give them something to resist in their outer life—a true vicious circle. This is one way in which people unconsciously create their own personal universe. Their lives become a self-fulfilling prophesy. Unfortunately, the universe they create isn't a happy one. On the other hand, you can always create a new one, at any time.

Based on our early-life interactions with our primary caretakers, we all develop beliefs and generalizations about who we are and what our relationship is to the rest of the world. I've mentioned before that we don't choose these beliefs, but instead soak them up from our primary caregivers, our teachers, and from others when we're too small to know any better. These beliefs become core components of the way we see ourselves, other people, and the world.

Your beliefs are critically important to your happiness for two reasons. First, the brain is a goal seeking mechanism, and a very powerful one. Your brain can (and does) make whatever you put into it come true in your life. Second, human beings have a powerful need for consistency between what they believe to be true and what really is true.

As has been said, people would rather be right than happy. This means that regardless of how much your beliefs misrepresent reality, or how much misery they create for you, you will arrange to be right about them by creating the circumstances that seem to confirm that what you believe is true.

Most people evaluate beliefs by whether they're true or false. If it's true it's worth believing, if it's false it isn't. This true-false distinction is not useful, despite the fact that we are so used to classifying things in this way. Why? Because *anything* you deeply believe comes true in reality; your brain is hard-wired to make this happen. So evaluating a belief by whether it is true or false is not useful. The useful way to evaluate beliefs is by whether they are *resourceful* or *non-resourceful* for you—by whether they create happiness and peace, or something else. Since whatever you deeply believe comes true, the only resourceful beliefs are those that contain an outcome you want.

The big secret is that you can *choose* what you want to believe— you don't have to believe what seems true based on past experience. The first step is to find out what these non-resourceful beliefs are. One way to begin to do this is to complete the following sentences:

I am _____.
People are _____.
The world is _____.

What we're looking for are the things you say to yourself when you're really down about things, when you're feeling the worst. We are *not* looking for what you learned in self-help books—those are things you think you *should* believe. We are not looking for "I am one with everything," "The world is filled with abundance," "People are basically good," "Everything happens for the best," and other platitudes you may agree with intellectually but really don't believe when the chips are down.

Instead, we're looking for what you really do believe about yourself, and say to yourself, about yourself, when things look darkest—things such as "I'm never going to be a success. No one will ever love me. There's something wrong with me. I can't seem to do anything right. People will take advantage of me if I don't watch them very carefully. Men always leave me in the end. No one cares about me. The world is dangerous and chaotic." These statements are important clues to what your negative core beliefs are.

The second way to determine what these beliefs are is even simpler: look at what is happening in your life. Because what you believe manifests in reality, you can tell what a person's beliefs are just by looking at the results they're getting. If you are having trouble sustaining a close relationship with the opposite sex, somewhere there is a core belief about you and the opposite sex that is creating that result. If you are having trouble with prosperity, or health, or any other issue, you must have a belief about that subject that is manifesting in what is actually happening for you. When you look at people who are getting better results, you can be sure that they have different, and more empowering, core beliefs on that subject. If they did not, they would not be getting different, and better, results.

Once you become aware of your core beliefs (and we're concerned with the negative beliefs here—the beliefs that are giving you the results you want don't need attention), the next step is to decide what would be a more empowering, resourceful belief. Then you can begin to adopt this new way of thinking about yourself. To do so, you have to start telling yourself this new belief over and over, and wiping the old one out of your mind whenever it pops up. The only reason the old belief seems true is that you've focused on it and experienced it so often, which of course makes it play out in reality, which then makes you focus on it more, which makes it play out in reality more. You see what I mean.

Focus on the new belief. Do it while meditating, driving, showering, anytime. Doing so may bring up old and uncomfortable feelings, so be prepared for that—the old belief will fight for its life (remember that it originated as part of your strategy for keeping yourself safe while growing up). Do not let the uncomfortable feelings bother you. Just keep focusing on what you want. Create an internal Technicolor movie of you getting just what you want and feeling happy and satisfied by it. The more vivid you can make this movie, the better. And, in addition to playing the movie during meditation, play it right before you go to sleep and right after waking up.

Most people who have had a significant negative emotional experience focus on what they do not want, such as abandonment (i.e., a repetition of the significant emotional experience). They have a rule: "Avoid 'x' at all costs!" and they spend a lot of energy scanning their environment to make sure "x" isn't lurking somewhere nearby.

When you notice yourself focusing on what you do not want, change the focus to what you do want. Since your brain always takes whatever you focus on as an instruction to make it happen, people who focus on what they do not want, ironically, end up getting it. To begin focusing on what you *do* want, when you've unconsciously and automatically focused on what you do not want for such a long time, takes effort and persistence. Allow for a learning curve. Learning to focus on what you want may take some time.

Earlier, I cited a second reason why beliefs come true: It is because we need consistency between what we believe and reality, and we will do anything to create this consistency. We create this consistency in three ways:

1. We attract, and are attracted to, people and situations that

confirm that what we believe is true. If you believe no one will ever really love you, you will somehow feel a magical attraction to men or women who *will* leave, even though consciously you have no way of knowing this about them in advance.

2. We find a way to see the belief as true even if it is not. In other words, we interpret behaviors of potential partners as meaning they will leave, are leaving, have left, etc., even if that isn't what their behavior really means. We put a meaning on whatever happens that confirms, in our mind, that our belief is true.

3. We act in such a way that people finally comply and really do act in the way we feared they would act. You fear he will leave and that fear causes you to act in such a way that he finally *does* leave.

With all three, you get to be right about what you believe. But isn't it better to be happy than right? Proving to yourself that beliefs that create suffering are true is a losing proposition.

The process of changing core beliefs can take several years to complete. Just identifying your core beliefs can take some time. But however long this process takes, it is worth doing. What we are talking about here is the difference between being an unconscious, automatic response mechanism, living out beliefs that create suffering, and being a conscious being who chooses what to believe based on the kind of world they want to live in.

You are already masterfully proficient at creating what you believe to be true and what you focus on. You have been unconsciously doing it all your life. Now, knowing that you can consciously direct your focus, and consciously decide what beliefs will serve you best, all you have to do is focus on what you want and you'll get it.

9. The Principle of the Neutral Universe

Everything in the universe is neutral. The words of Hamlet are true:
"There is nothing either good or bad, but thinking makes it so."

You give everything in your world meaning. You interpret everything you come into contact with according to your map of reality. Unless you know better, your good-bad interpretations feel like the truth. It is easy to forget that nothing has any *intrinsic* meaning and that *you* have assigned qualities and meanings that seem to be inherent to the people and things in your life.

Different people and different cultures assign value to different things. The same object, idea, or occurrence can be welcomed in one culture and feared in another. Realizing this, you can create the world you want just by assigning meaning in whatever way you like. Make everything good, and the world is good; make everything bad, and the world is bad.

As you already know: It's okay to play Hamlet, but don't fall into the trap of thinking you *are* Hamlet. If you know you are just playing, you can have fun with it. You can approach your life in a spirit of curiosity and discovery, of humor and experimentation. After all, you are the creator of your reality. And you can change it.

This is not a way of saying that you have no obligation to act responsibly or honestly or that anything you do is okay because there is no right or wrong. This is not an argument for situational ethics. Behaving toward others as you would want them to behave toward you is still and always will be the best policy. Conscious people realize that all thoughts, all actions, have consequences.

The universe really is neutral, which when you think about it, is a great thing for you. It is a blank canvas on which you can write your own story. Always remember that you have enormous power, and with this power you can create whatever life you want, as long as you are willing to do the work to become conscious and to make the choices that bring happiness and inner peace. Since nothing has any intrinsic meaning, and you give everything any and all the meaning it has, your only choice is whether to accept the unconscious meanings assigned to you before you knew any better, along with their consequences, or to create whatever meaning—and therefore whatever life—you want. Once you begin to exercise this power, I promise you will never go back!

The Anti-Quiet Culture

ⓖ

One last thought. We live in a culture prejudiced against stillness, opposed to motionlessness. We live in an anti-quiet culture. We worship movement, activity, noise. That's what gets our attention. We do not usually equate stillness with progress and growth, and do not generally think there is much to be gained by being still. There does not seem to be much to learn from quietness or from waiting. Without stimuli—for our eyes, ears, mouths—what is there?

When was the last time you heard someone say, "I'm really proud of my son. Yesterday, he sat in his room all day, alone, and deeply contemplated life?" Most parents would be worried. "When is he going to quit sitting around and get a job?" We worship activity. Do something! Move! Say something! Are we afraid that if we remain still for more than a moment that we somehow court the Grim Reaper? We think, "We've got a lot to do before we die, and maybe if we look busy enough—alive enough—death will leave us alone and not interrupt us."

Don't get me wrong—I'm one of the most action-oriented people you will ever meet. But before Holosync, my actions and goals were unconscious and a result of my generally futile attempts to deal with my suffering, even though I did not realize what I was doing. Now my actions and goals are conscious and the result of a deep stillness inside that allows me to see more clearly what needs doing, to remain unattached to the outcome, and do whatever needs doing in a way that (I certainly hope) benefits me and benefits those around me. To me, this is being alive.

Gandhi once said of Western culture, "Here are people with everything, except stillness." Stillness is not death. Stillness allows room for feeling, sensing, experiencing, knowing. Stillness creates space—a sacred space, if you will—in which we connect with the very life we are. Stillness allows the development of the Witness, which as we have seen, is the doorway to happiness and inner peace.

This stillness is not a sensory experience in the way most of us know it. It is deeper. It is an awareness, a *centeredness*. One partici-pant in the Centerpointe program described it this way: "When meditating with my Holosync soundtracks I feel as though I'm in touch with my own humanity in the most metaphysical and pro-found sense. The world, as I've built it in my head, settles and disappears. And I know what peace feels like."

Meditation is oil upon the rushing waters of our high-velocity lifestyles. As T.S. Eliot writes in the poem that began this chapter, "I said to my soul, be still and wait…" and "the darkness shall be the light, and the stillness the dancing." What we most desire is already within us. Our job is to be quiet and wait.

APPENDIX I

The Science Behind Holosync and Other Neurotechnologies

A Revolution in Neuroscience: Tuning the Brain

⑥

S cience ushered in a new era in our ability to learn, be creative, remember, control our moods, reduce stress, resolve unwanted behavior patterns, and a host of other desirable ends, with the appearance of a remarkable paper by Dr. Gerald Oster, of Mt. Sinai Medical Center, in the October 1973 issue of *Scientific American*.

Oster's paper, entitled "Auditory Beats in the Brain," described how pulsations called binaural beats occurred in the brain when tones of different frequencies were presented separately to each ear. As a result, the entire brain became entrained to a frequency equal to the difference between the two tones and began to resonate to that frequency. In other words, Oster discovered a method for what is called *entrainment* of brain wave patterns. (1)

Simultaneously, Robert Monroe, of the Monroe Institute of

Applied Sciences, was also investigating binaural beats. In thousands of experiments, using an EEG machine to monitor subjects' electrical brain wave patterns, Monroe also concluded that he could entrain brain wave patterns using binaural beats. In addition, he noted that the response did not happen only in the area of the brain responsible for hearing, or only in one hemisphere or the other, but rather, the entire brain resonated. The waveforms of both hemispheres exhibited identical frequencies, amplitude, phase, and coherence.

Since then, many researchers have verified this phenomenon. Language and speech pathologist Dr. Suzanne Evans Morris, Ph.D., reports

> Research supports the theory that different frequencies presented to each ear through stereo headphones . . . create a difference tone (or binaural beat) as the brain puts together the two tones it actually hears. Through EEG monitoring the difference tone is identified by a change in the electrical pattern produced by the brain. For example, frequencies of 200 Hz and 210 Hz produce a binaural beat frequency of 10 Hz. Monitoring of the brain's electricity (EEG) shows that the brain produces increased 10 Hz activity with equal frequency and amplitude of the wave form in both hemispheres. (2)

Research by Dr. Lester Fehmi, director of the Princeton Behavioral Medicine and Biofeedback Clinic, and perhaps the foremost authority on hemispheric synchronization in the brain, also confirms that hemispheric synchronization and brain entrainment can be induced by binaural beats. (3)

Dr. Arthur Hastings, Ph.D., in a paper entitled "Tests of the Sleep Induction Technique" describes the effects of subjects listening to a cassette tape specially engineered to create binaural beats in the brain. In this case, the sounds on the tape were designed to slow the brain wave patterns from a normal waking *beta* brain wave pattern to a slower *alpha* pattern, then to a still slower *theta* pattern (the brain wave pattern of dreaming sleep), and finally to a *delta* pattern, the slowest of all, the brainwave pattern of dreamless sleep. Hastings says:

> We were able to test the effects of the sleep tape on brain waves with an EEG machine through the courtesy of the researchers at the Langely-Porter Neuropsychiatric Institute,

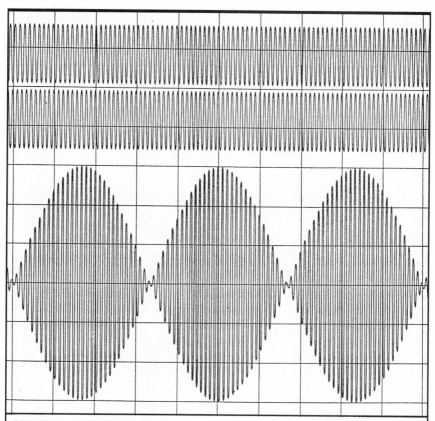

SINE WAVES COMBINE TO PRODUCE BEATS in this illustration based on oscilloscope traces. The two waves at the top are of slightly different frequency; when they are combined, the resulting wave at the bottom varies slowly in amplitude. The variations are beats and would be perceived acoustically as modulations in loudness. If the two signals were presented separately to each ear, binaural beats would be heard. These differ in character from monaural, or ordinary, beats and are generated within the brain.

"Auditory Beats in the Brain" by Gerald Oster. Scientific American, Oct. 1973, (used with permission).

part of the University of California Medical School in San Francisco. Dr. Joe Kaniya, Director of the Psychophysiology of Consciousness Laboratory, monitored the brain-wave frequencies of one subject as he listened to the sleep tape.

The chart recording showed a typical sleep onset pattern: initial alpha waves, then a slowing of the brain waves with sleep spindles, and finally a pattern of stage 2 and 3 sleep brain waves in the low theta range . . . the patterns in the various stages suggested that the tape was influencing the subject's state. (4)

Dr. Bill D. Schul also refers to the phenomenon of brain entrainment:

[P]hased sine waves at discernible sound frequencies, when blended to create 'beat' frequencies within the ranges of electrical brain waves found at the various stages of human sleep, will create a frequency following response (FFR) within the EEG pattern of the individual listening to such audio waveforms. The FFR in turn evokes physiological and mental states in direct relationship to the original stimulus. With the availability of this tool, it becomes possible to develop and hold the subject into any of the various stages of sleep, from light Alpha relaxation through Theta into Delta and in REM (dreaming). (5)

Schul concluded that "Binaural beat-frequency stimulation creates a sustaining FFR that is synchronous in both amplitude and frequency between the brain hemispheres. (5)

F. Holmes Atwater of the Monroe Institute describes the neurophysics of the binaural beat brain entrainment process:

Within the sound processing centers of the brain, pulse stimulation provides relevant information to the higher centers of the brain. In the case of a wave form phase differ-ence the electron pulse rate in one part of a sound-process-ing center is greater than in another. The differences in electron pulse stimulation within the sound processing centers of the brain are an anomaly. This anomaly (the difference in electron pulse stimulation) comes and goes as the two different frequency wave forms mesh in and out of phase. As a result of these constantly increasing and decreas-ing differences in electron pulse stimulation, an amplitude modulated standing wave (the binaural beat) is generated within the sound processing centers of the brain itself. It is this standing wave which acts to entrain brain waves. (6)

Atwater further states, "A conventional binaural beat generates two amplitude modulated standing waves, one in each hemi-sphere's olivary nucleus. Such binaural beats will entrain both hemi-spheres to the same frequency, establishing equivalent electromagnetic environments and maximizing interhemispheric neural communica-tion" (6).

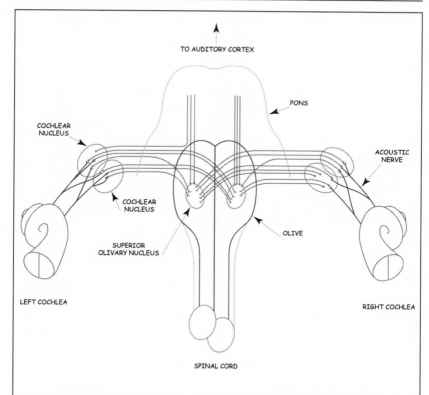

TO AUDITORY CORTEX

PONS

COCHLEAR
NUCLEUS

ACOUSTIC
NERVE

COCHLEAR
NUCLEUS

OLIVE

SUPERIOR
OLIVARY NUCLEUS

LEFT COCHLEA

RIGHT COCHLEA

SPINAL CORD

LOWER AUDITORY CENTERS of the brain are in the medulla oblongata, viewed here schematically from the back of the neck. Nerve impulses from the right and left ears first meet in the left or right superior olivary nucleus. These structures are part of the olive, an organ that in this view lies behind the brain stem. It is probable that binaural beats are detected here.

"Auditory Beats in the Brain" by Gerald Oster. Scientific American, Oct. 1973, (used with permission).

Not Just a Pretty Picture

The ability to entrain brain wave patterns opens up an exciting world of mind-boggling possibilities. Researchers in neuroscience could not contain their excitement.

"It's difficult to try to responsibly convey some sense of excitement about what's going on," said UCLA neurophysiologist John Kiebeskind. "You find yourself sounding like people you don't respect. You try to be more conservative and not say such wild and intriguing things, but damn! The field is wild and intriguing. It's hard to avoid talking that way...We are at a frontier, and it's a terribly exciting time to be in this line of work" (7).

Neurochemist Candace Pert, of the National Institute of Mental Health, had this to say:

> There's a revolution going on. There used to be two systems of knowledge: hard science—chemistry, physics, biophysics—on the one hand, and, on the other, a system of knowledge that included ethology, psychology, and psychiatry. And now it's as if a lightning bolt had connected the two. It's all one system neuroscience . . .The present era in neuroscience is comparable to the time when Louis Pasteur first found out that germs cause disease. (8)

David Krech, Ph.D., a University of California at Berkeley psychologist, predicted almost twenty-five years ago: "I foresee the day when we shall have the means, and therefore, inevitably, the temptation, to manipulate the behavior and intellectual functioning of all people through environmental and biochemical manipulation of the brain." (9)

That day may very well be here now, and the gentle altering of brain wave patterns using sound may be the easiest, most potent, and safest way to do it. Centerpointe Research Institute currently uses a sound technology called Holosync® to entrain brain wave patterns, giving us the ability to influence or create tranquility, pain control, creativity, euphoria, excitement, focused attention, relief from stress, enhanced learning ability, enhanced problem-solving ability, increased memory, accelerated healing, behavior modification, and improvements in mental and emotional health.

Michael Hutchison, in his book *Megabrain Power,* sums up this revolution in neuroscience: ". . .[N]ew breakthroughs in neuroscience and microelectronics have permitted scientists to 'map' the electrical and chemical activity of the brain in action. Scientists have used the new technology to monitor the brains of those meditators, artists, and other rare individuals who are able to enter peak domains at will and to map their brain activity during those peak states." (10)

According to Hutchison, these scientists' first findings were that those peak states are not mysterious and unpredictable phenomena, but are clearly linked to specific patterns of brain activity. These patterns include dramatic changes in brain wave activity, hemispheric symmetry, and rapid alterations in the levels of various neurochemicals. If we could learn to produce these patterns of brain activity, they reasoned, we should be able to produce the peak states they are associated with. ". . .They found that by using types of mechanical stimulation, such as . . . precise combinations of pulsating sound waves...they could actually produce those same 'peak state' brain patterns in ordinary people . . . " (10)

The Well-Balanced Brain
ⓖ

Just as we exercise our bodies to feel better and improve our physical health, stimulating the brain in this manner "exercises" the brain, bringing better mental and emotional health and increased intellectual functioning. Researcher Robert Cosgrove, Jr., Ph.D., M.D., and an authority in pharmaceutics and biomedical engineering, noted that technologies that alter brainwave patterns

> . . . with appropriately selected stimulation protocols [have] been observed by us to be an excellent neuro-pathway exerciser. As such we believe it has great potential for use in promoting optimal cerebral performance . . . Furthermore, the long-term effects of regular use . . . on maintaining and improving cerebral performance throughout life and possibly delaying for decades the deterioration of the brain traditionally associated with aging is very exciting. (11)

There are four categories of brain wave patterns. The most rapid brain wave pattern is that of beta, from about 14 Hz to more than 100 Hz. This is the pattern of normal waking consciousness, and it is associated with concentration, arousal, alertness, and cognition, while at higher levels, beta is associated with anxiety. As we become more relaxed, the brain wave activity slows into the alpha range, from 8 to 13.9 Hz. These are the brain wave patterns of deep relaxation, and of what has been called the *twilight state* between sleep and waking, while the higher end of alpha represents a more relaxed yet focused state.

Slower still are theta waves, between 4 and 7.9 Hz. This is the state of dreaming sleep and also of increased creativity, superlearning, integrative experiences, and increased memory. The slowest brain wave pattern is delta, that of dreamless sleep, below 4 Hz. Generally people are asleep in delta, but there is evidence that it is possible to remain alert in this state—a very deep trance-like, nonphysical state. It is in delta that our brains are triggered to release

Four Categories of Brain Wave Patterns	
beta (14–100 Hz)	Concentration, arousal, alertness, cognition Higher levels associated with anxiety, dis-ease, feelings of separation, fight or flight
alpha (8–13.9 Hz)	Relaxation, superlearning, relaxed focus, light trance Increased serontonin production Pre-sleep or pre-waking drowsiness Mediation, beginning of access to unconscious mind
theta (4–7.9 Hz)	Dreaming sleep (REM sleep) Increased production of catecholamines (vital for learning and memory), increased creativity Integrative, emotional experiences, potential change in behavior, increased retention of learned material Hypnagogic imagery, trance, deep mediation, access to unconscious mind
delta (.1–3.9 Hz)	Dreamless sleep Human growth hormone released Deep, trance-like, non-physical state, loss of body awareness Access to unconscious and "collective unconscious" mind, greatest "push" to brain when induced with Holosync®

large quantities of healing growth hormone (12).

As we slow the brain wave patterns from beta to alpha to theta to delta, there is a corresponding increase in balance between the two hemispheres of the brain. This more balanced brain state is called brain synchrony, or brain synchronization. This balancing phenomenon was noted in early EEG studies of experienced meditators in the 1970s. In deep meditative states, their brain waves shifted from the usual asymmetrical patterns, with one hemisphere dominant over the other, to a balanced state of whole-brain integration, with the same brain wave frequency throughout. As we will see, various mental abilities and experiences are induced naturally in these different brain wave patterns, and many of these abilities and experiences are quite remarkable.

Robert Monroe of the Monroe Institute reported that inducing brain wave patterns through the creation of binaural beats in the brain caused a wide range of effects, including "focusing of attention, suggestibility, problem solving, creativity, memory, and learning . . . sleep induction, pain control . . . and enhanced learning . . ." (13).

Other scientists have noted that these slower brain wave patterns are accompanied by deep tranquility, flashes of creative insight, euphoria, intensely focused attention, and enhanced learning abilities. Dr. Lester Fehmi, director of the Princeton Biofeedback Research Institute, has said that hemispheric synchronization represents "the maximum efficiency of information transport through the whole brain" and "[it] is correlated experientially with a union with experience, and 'into-it-ness.' Instead of feeling separate and narrow-focused, you tend to feel more into it—that is, unified with the experience, you are the experience—and the scope of your awareness is widened a great deal, so that you're including many more experiences at the same time. There's a whole-brain sensory integration going on, and it's as if you become less self-conscious and you function more intuitively." (14)

Super-Learning

One of the observed effects of this type of sound-induced brain synchronization is increased learning ability. What is now known as *superlearning* began in the late 1960s and early 1970s with the work of Bulgarian psychiatrist Georgi Lozanov. Lozanov used deep relaxation combined with synchronized rhythms in the brain to cause students to produce alpha waves. He found that students when in this state learned over five times as much information with less study time per day, with greater long-term retention. In some cases, as much as thirty times as much was learned.

Speech-Language pathologist Suzanne Evans Morris, Ph.D., describes the relationship between different brainwave patterns and learning, as well as other related states such as concentration, problem solving, receptivity, and creativity.

Receptivity for learning is related to specific states of consciousness. Predominant brainwave patterns are associated with different states of consciousness or awareness. For example, beta frequencies ranging from 13–26 Hz are associated with concentration, and alert problem solving; alpha frequencies (8–13 Hz) occur when the eyes are closed and a state of alert relaxation is present; theta (4–7 Hz) is associated with deep relaxation with a high receptivity for new experiences and learning . . . (15)

Morris also describes how recordings containing binaural beat signals can be used to "create the ability to sustain this theta period of openness for learning." (15)

Morris goes on to say that "[t]he introduction of theta signals . . . into the learning environment theoretically allows for a broader and deeper processing of the information provided by the teacher . . . [and] increases . . . focus of attention and creates a mental set of open receptivity." She notes that in the use of such binaural beat signals in a classroom setting, children exhibited "improved focus of attention" and "a greater openness and enthusiasm for learning." (15)

Morris further describes what happens in the brain that makes this type of accelerated learning so effective:

The presence of theta patterns (4–7 Hz) in the brain has been associated with states of increased receptivity for learning and reduced filtering of information by the left hemisphere. This state of awareness is available for relatively brief periods as the individual enters a state of reverie or passes in and out of the deep sleep phase of the 90 minute sleep cycle. [Binaural beat] signals, however, can facilitate a prolonged state of theta to produce a relaxed receptivity for learning . . . [These signals] create a state of coherence in the brain. Right and left hemispheres as well as subcortical areas become activated in harmony, reflected by equal frequency and amplitude of EEG patterns from both hemispheres. This creates an internal physiological environment for learning which involves the whole brain. The linear, sequential style of problem solving preferred by the left hemisphere is brought into balance with the global, intuitive style of the right hemisphere and limbic system (subcortex). This allows the learner to have greater access to internal and external knowledge and provides a milieu for expanding intuition in problem solving. One of the by-products of hemispheric synchronization appears to be a highly focused state of attending. The ability to reduce 'mind chatter' and focus the attention is critical for efficient learning (16).

Binaural beat signals have been used in the classroom to enhance learning ability. Teachers in the Tacoma, Washington, public schools, under the direction of psychologist Devon Edrington, used audio tapes containing a binaural beat sound technology to influence the learning ability of students. They found that students who were taught, studied, and took tests while these tapes were playing did significantly better than a control group not using the tapes. (17)

The theta state also seems to be one where behavior and belief system changes can more easily be made. Suzanne Evans Morris discusses the work of neurotechnology and biofeedback researcher Thomas Budzynski, (1981) in which he described the theta state as

> . . . a transition zone between wakefulness and sleep in which one can absorb new information in an uncritical, non-analytical fashion. [Budzynski] speculated that this allows new information to be considered by the right hemisphere through bypassing the critical filters of the left hemisphere. Thus, information leading to a change in self-concept would become more available; modification of habitual behaviors or consideration of one's belief system could occur more easily if alternatives were presented during a period of theta activity. (18)

Medical researcher Dr. Gene W. Brockopp also believes behavior modification is enhanced when the subject can be placed in slower, more receptive brain wave patterns. He speculates that using technology to induce brain wave changes can

> . . . actively induce a state of deactivation in which the brain is passive, but not asleep; awake, but not involved with the 'clutter' of an ongoing existence. If this is true, then it may be a state in which new cognitive strategies could be designed and developed . . . . [i]f we can help a person to experience different brain-wave states consciously through driving them with external stimulation, we may facilitate the individual's ability to allow more variations in their functioning through breaking up patterns at the neural level. This may help them develop the ability to shift gears or 'shuttle' and move them away from habit patterns of behavior to become more flexible and creative, and to develop elegant strategies of functioning (19).

Many other researchers have described the benefits of alpha and theta brain wave states. Budzynski has done extensive research on learning and suggestion when the brain is in a theta state. Theta, Budzynski suggested, is the state in which superlearning takes place—when in theta, people are able to learn new languages, accept suggestions for changes in behavior and attitudes, or memorize large amounts of information. He says, "We take advantage of the fact that the hypnagogic [theta] state, the twilight state . . . has these properties of uncritical acceptance of verbal material, or almost any material it can process." In this state, Budzynski says, "a lot of work gets done very quickly." (20, 21)

Budzynski and psychobiologist Dr. James McGaugh of the University of California at Irvine have both found that information is also more easily processed and recalled in a theta state. Noted researchers Elmer and Alyce Green, of the Menninger Foundation, have also studied this phenomenon, finding that memories experienced in a theta state "were not like going through a memory in one's mind but rather like an experience, a reliving." Individuals producing theta waves also had "new and valid ideas or synthesis of ideas, not primarily by deduction but springing by intuition from unconscious sources."

In their seminal book, *Beyond Biofeedback*, the Greens further discussed many remarkable effects of the theta brain wave state. They found that those producing theta waves became highly creative. They had life-altering insights, what the Greens called "integrative experiences leading to feelings of psychological well-being." On psychological tests, subjects scored as being "psychologically healthier, had more social poise, were less rigid and conforming, and were more self-accepting and creative." Another remarkable effect was that these subjects became very healthy. Emotionally, these people had "improved relationships with other people as well as greater tolerance, understanding, and love of oneself and of one's world" (22).

Alpha and theta states have also been shown to facilitate addiction recovery. Dr. Eugene Peniston and Dr. Paul Kulkosky, of the University of Southern Colorado, trained a group of alcoholics to enter the alpha and theta states. These alcoholics showed a recovery rate many orders of magnitude greater than a control group. Thirteen months later, this alpha-theta group showed "sustained prevention of relapse," and these findings were confirmed in follow-up study three years later. In addition, this group showed a marked personality transformation, including significant increases in qualities such as warmth, stability, conscientiousness, boldness, imaginativeness, and self-control, along with decreases in depression and anxiety. (23)

At the brain wave pattern at the juncture between the alpha and theta rhythms, often called the *crossover point* by neuroscientists, subjects have experienced some remarkable changes. Houston therapist William Beckwith has reported that in his clients the experience of this crossover point is often accompanied by "the seemingly miraculous resolutions of complex psychological problems." (24)

Other studies have suggested that states of brain synchronization increase memory. McGaugh's research on memory and theta waves showed that "the more theta waves appeared in an animal's EEG after a training session, the more it remembered. This was true in all cases . . . Apparently, the best predictor of memory was the amount of theta waves recorded in the animal's brain. [Theta waves] show that the brain is in the right state to process and store information." (25)

Scientists have discovered that for memories to form, the brain must undergo a process called long-term potentiation (LTP), involving electrical and chemical changes in the neurons associated with memory. Without LTP, incoming information is not stored, but rather quickly and totally forgotten. Neurophysiologist Dr. Gary Lynch and associates at the University of California at Irvine discovered that the key to LTP is the theta brain wave pattern. "We have found the magic rhythm that makes LTP. There's a magic rhythm, the theta rhythm." According to Lynch, this is the natural rhythm of the hippocampus, the part of the brain essential for the formation and storage of new memories and the recall of old memories (26).

Other studies have confirmed the incredible benefits of the theta state. In experiments conducted at the Monroe Institute of Applied Science, subjects who produced theta waves (as measured on an EEG) in response to binaural beats "invariably emerged from the experience reporting all the mental phenomena associated with the theta state, such as vivid hypnagogic imagery, creative thoughts, integrative experiences, and spontaneous memories" (27).

How do these amazing mental and emotional changes take place? Many researchers believe that different brain wave patterns are linked to the production in the brain of various neurochemicals associated with relaxation and stress release, increased learning and creativity, memory, and other desirable benefits. These neurochemicals include beta-endorphins, acetylcholine, vasopressin, and serotonin.

Dr. Margaret Patterson, in collaboration with biochemist Dr. Ifor Capel, at the Marie Curie Cancer Memorial Foundation Research Department, in Surrey, England, has shown that certain frequencies in the brain dramatically speed up production of a variety of neurotransmitters, different frequencies triggering different brain chemicals. For instance, a 10 Hz (alpha) brain wave pattern boosts the production and turnover rate of serotonin, a chemical messenger that increases relaxation and eases pain, while catecholamines, vital for memory and learning, respond at around 4 Hz (theta).

According to Capel, ". . . as far as we can tell, each brain center generates impulses at a specific frequency based on the predominant neurotransmitter it secretes. In other words, the brain's internal communication system—its language, if you like—is based on frequency . . . Presumably, when we send in waves of electrical energy at, say, 10 Hz, certain cells in the lower brain stem will respond because they normally fire within that frequency range." (28)

Dr. William Bauer, one of the foremost experts in the field of electromedicine, elaborates:

> What I think is happening . . . is that by sending out the proper frequency, proper waveform and proper current . . . we tend to change the configuration of the cell membrane. Cells that are at sub-optimal levels are stimulated to 'turn on' and produce what they're supposed to produce, probably through DNA, which is stimulated through the cell membrane . . . You're charging the cells through a biochemical process that can possibly balance the acetylcholine or whatever neurotransmitter needs to be turned on . . . (29)

The increased production of these different neurochemicals can greatly enhance memory and learning. A research team at the Veterans Administration Hospital in Palo Alto found that a group of normal human subjects, when given substances that increased acetylcholine production in the brain, showed great improvement in long-term memory, while at MIT, students taking acetylcholine enhancers experienced improved memory and increased ability to learn lists of words. (30) Researcher Lester A. Henry noted that acetylcholine "is essential to such higher mental processes as learning and memory." (31)

Recent studies show that insufficient acetylcholine causes

memory loss and reduces learning and intelligence. Lack of acetylcholine been linked in part to confusion and memory loss in patients Alzheimer's disease (32, 33). Other studies have shown that when individuals are given substances that increase the amount of acetylcholine, they show significant increases in scores on memory and intelligence tests (34, 35).

Acetylcholine has also been associated with a greater number of neurons in the cortex and also with greater brain size, with humans having the highest density of acetylcholine in the brain. UC Berkeley researcher Mark Rosenzweig has shown a direct connection between acetylcholine and intelligence. (36)

Other neurochemicals that are produced in the brain in response to binaural beats have been associated with increased memory, learning, and other benefits. Men in their fifties taking vasopressin, a neurochemical closely related to the endorphins, showed significant improvement in memory, leaning, and reaction time. In another study, sixteen normal, healthy subjects of average intelligence were given vasopressin several times, after which they showed dramatic improvement in their ability to learn and remember. (37) Dutch scientists further found that vasopressin had a long-term "cementing effect on consolidation of information." (38)

At the National Institute of Mental Health (NIMH), research has indicated that vasopressin boosts memory, enabling subjects to "chunk" and encode information better. (Chunking refers to the ability to group large amounts of information together into more easily remembered bits). NIMH found that decreasing vasopressin is associated with memory deficits. Vasopressin is also associated with and enhances production of theta waves that are associated with increased access to memories and increased creativity. Vasopressin also stimulates the release of endorphins and has restored memory in amnesia victims (39, 40).

The Endorphin Connection

Scientists have also found that the endorphins released when the brain is exposed to alpha and theta binaural beat patterns enhance many mental functions. Endorphins have a powerful strengthening effect on learning and memory, for instance, and have been known to reverse amnesia. Researcher David de Weid found that rats injected with endorphins remembered things longer. Dr. Andrew Schally, 1977 winner of the Nobel Prize for medicine, found that rats receiving injections of endorphins showed improved maze-running abilities. (41)

Why do endorphins increase learning and memory? Neuroscientists believe that in humans the places in the brain that produce the most endorphins, and contain the greatest concentration of endorphin receptors, are the same areas of the brain involved most intimately with learning and memory. Dr. Aryeh Routtenberg, of Northwestern University, located these pleasure centers in the brain and noted

> [T]he evidence clearly shows that the brain reward pathways play an important role in learning and memory . . . I have speculated that the pathways of brain reward may function as the pathways of memory consolidation. By this I mean that when something is learned, activity in the brain reward pathways facilitates formation of memory. . . . Evidence for the reward effects of localized electrical stimulation . . . and for the association of reward paths with memory formation indicates that the neural substrates of self-stimulation play a vital role in the guidance of behavior. (42)

Scientists now know of at least seven chemicals in the endorphin family that have effects on memory and learning. Endorphins, according to neuroscientists, "serve as the body's 'natural reward system,' providing us with a rush of pleasure whenever we learn something or act in some way that is conducive to our survival as a species." (43) This means that new belief systems designed to effect desirable behavior changes, if presented to the mind when it is flooded with endorphins, may be perceived as beneficial and adopted as such—a powerful boost to any behavior modification protocol.

Dr. Candice Pert of NIMH, the discoverer of the opiate receptor, has also described this process, noting that "the endorphins, our natural opiates, are a filtering mechanism in the brain. The opiate system selectively filters incoming information from every sense— sight, hearing, smell, taste, and touch—and blocks some of it from percolating up to higher levels of consciousness." (44)

Scientists now believe that the moment when learning takes place—the "aha" moment—is that moment when a particular reality has been selected and filtered by our endorphins and is suddenly apprehended by our brain in such a way that we learn something new. This learning being rewarded by a flood of endorphins along our pleasure-learning pathways. (45)

The production in the brain of alpha and theta patterns is also correlated with the *relaxation response*—the mirror image of the more well known fight or flight response. The fight or flight response takes blood flow away from the brain and toward the periphery of the body, floods the bloodstream with sugar, and increases heart rate, blood pressure, and respiration rate in order to prepare one for defense or flight. In this state, learning ability, as well as other mental functions including problem solving and reasoning ability, are inhibited.

The relaxation response, on the other hand, mobilizes us for inward activity by reducing heart rate and blood pressure, relaxing muscles, and increasing the percentage of oxygen flowing to the brain. As one might expect, the fight or flight response is accompanied by low-amplitude, high-frequency beta brain wave patterns, while the relaxation response, so beneficial to learning and problem solving, is accompanied by high amplitude, low frequency alpha and theta rhythms. (46, 47) When we use sound technologies to induce these slower brain wave patterns, we also induce the relaxation response, another possible reason for the increases in learning ability noted by so many researchers.

The Effect on Hormones

A recent study performed by Dr. Vincent Giampapa, M.D., former president of the American Board of Anti-Aging Medicine, revealed that placing a listener in the alpha, theta, and delta brain wave patterns using Holosync audio technology dramatically affects production of three important hormones related to both increased longevity and well-being: cortisol, DHEA, and melatonin.

Cortisol is a hormone produced by the adrenal glands. According to Dr. Giampapa, cortisol is the major age-accelerating hormone within the brain. It also interferes with learning and memory and has, in general, negative effects on health and well being.

DHEA is also produced by the adrenal glands. It is a precursor, or source ingredient, to virtually every hormone the body needs. DHEA levels are a key determinant of physiological age and resistance to disease. When DHEA levels are low, we are more susceptible to aging and disease; when they are high, the body is at its peak—vibrant, healthy, and able to effectively combat disease. DHEA acts as a buffer against stress-related hormones (such as cortisol), which is why as you get older and make less DHEA you are more susceptible to stress and disease.

A study published in the *New England Journal of Medicine* (December 11, 1986) found that a 100 microgram per deciliter increase in DHEA blood levels corresponded with a 48% reduction in mortality due to cardiovascular disease—and a 36% reduction in mortality for any reason.

Melatonin is a hormone associated with the creation of restful sleep. We make less of it as we age, and since during sleep many important rejuvenating substances are created in the brain, the inability to sleep soundly can dramatically decrease the quality of your life and greatly accelerate aging.

Dr. Giampapa found the following changes in levels of melatonin, DHEA, and cortisol in 19 users of Holosync audio technology listening four hours a day over a three-day period:

- Over 68% had increases in DHEA levels, with an average increase of 43.77%. Several participants had increases of 50, 60, even 90%.
- Cortisol was down an average of 46.47%, with positive changes in 68% of the people, and with several participants having decreases of 70 or 80%.
- Melatonin levels increased an average of 97.77%, with positive changes happening in over 73% of the participants. Many had improvements of 100, 200, even 300%.

Pushing the Brain to Change

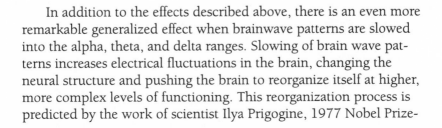

In addition to the effects described above, there is an even more remarkable generalized effect when brainwave patterns are slowed into the alpha, theta, and delta ranges. Slowing of brain wave patterns increases electrical fluctuations in the brain, changing the neural structure and pushing the brain to reorganize itself at higher, more complex levels of functioning. This reorganization process is predicted by the work of scientist Ilya Prigogine, 1977 Nobel Prize-winner in chemistry.

Prigogine's work has been applied to all changes in all kinds of open systems—everything from a seed germinating, to a corporation expanding, a highway system growing, a cell dividing, or a human being experiencing behavioral or emotional changes.

The human brain is the ultimate open system, constantly exchanging energy with its environment. Up to a point, the system can handle all kinds of fluctuations. But if the input becomes too much, the system is pushed past its limits and the system reorganizes itself at a higher order. A runner, for instance, gives more physical input to his body than it can handle, and it responds by reorganizing itself at a higher level that can handle this increased input—which we call "getting in shape."

Using binaural beat technology to change brain wave patterns causes a similar effect in the brain. The alpha, theta, and delta brain wave patterns are states of great fluctuation in the brain. A graphic representation of these brain wave patterns shows that the amplitude (the height of the waveform) increases as we move from alpha to theta to delta. In other words, the amount of fluctuation increases. These increased fluctuations are more than the nervous system can handle with its current structure, and the brain responds by reorganizing itself at a higher, more complex level of functioning. It does this by creating new neural pathways within itself, creating increased communication between parts of the brain that previously were not communicating. This is the balance, or synchrony, between the two hemispheres of the brain discussed at the beginning of this appendix. This synchrony brings with it many remarkable changes. As noted earlier, Lester Fehmi, of the Princeton Biofeedback Research Institute, has stated that "synchrony represents the maximum efficiency of information transport through the whole brain." (49)

As demonstrated earlier in this paper, there are two main effects of reorganization and increased synchrony in the brain. One is an increase in various mental capabilities: increased learning ability, creativity, mental clarity, intelligence, intuition, and so on. Second, each time the neural structure changes, positive changes in mental and emotional health occur. As the brain reorganizes at the next level of functioning, the subject's model of the world changes with it. With the creation of new neural pathways, connections are perceived between bits of information that previously seemed unrelated, and more choices are available. Herein lies the theoretical explanation for the amazing personality changes that researchers have reported in subjects using sound technology similar to Holosync to change brain wave patterns.

Clearly we are on the frontier of a marvelous new field with untold possibilities. The ability to map and entrain brain waves, and the states they represent, gives us a powerful new tool to effect human change and growth. It has been shown that induced brain wave states can cause superlearning, increased creativity, induce sleep, control pain, modify behavior, focus attention, relieve stress, increase memory, and dramatically improve mental and emotional health. Centerpointe Research Institute is proud to be at the forefront of this new and exciting field. We invite you to join us as we leap into the 21st century.

BIBLIOGRAPHY

1. Oster, Gerald. "Auditory beats in the brain." *Scientific American*, 229, 94–102. 1973.

2. Morris, Suzanne. *The Facilitation of Learning*. Privately published manuscript, p. 15. 1989.

3. Hutchison, Michael. *Megabrain*. Ballantine Books: New York, p. 219. 1986 .

4. Hastings, Arthur. *Tests of the Sleep Induction Technique*. Privately published manuscript, 1975.

5. Schul, Bill. Conceptual discussion of work plan, Monroe Institute of Applied Sciences, Faber, Virginia, 1986, p. 9–10.

6. Atwater, F. *The Monroe Institute's Hemi-Sync Process, A Theoretical Perspective*. The Monroe Institute of Applied Sciences, 1988. pp. 4, 7.

7. Quoted by Michael Hutchison. *Megabrain*. Ballantine Books: New York, 1986, p. 2.

8. Quoted by Michael Hutchison. *Megabrain*. Ballantine Books: New York, 1986, p. 2.

9. Bylinski, Gene. *Mood Control*. NY: Scribner, 1978.

10. Hutchison, Michael. *Megabrain Power*. New York: Hyperion, 1994. pp. 22–23.

11. Quoted in Hutchison, Michael. *Megabrain Power*. New York: Hyperion, 1994. p. 89.

12. Hutchison, *Megabrain Power*. New York: Hyperion, 1994. p. 33.

13. Hutchison, Michael. *Megabrain*. Ballantine Books: New York, 1986, p. 25.

14. Fehmi, Lester F., and George Fritz. "Open Focus: The Attentional Foundation of Health and Well-Being." *Somatics*, Spring 1980.

15. Morris, Suzanne. *The Facilitation of Learning*. Privately published manuscript, 1989, p. 16.

16. Morris, Suzanne. *The Facilitation of Learning*. Privately published manuscript, 1989, p. 16–17.

17. Edrington, Devon. *A Palliative for Wandering Attention*. Unpublished manuscript, 1984.

18. Morris, Suzanne. *The Facilitation of Learning*. Privately published manuscript, 1989, p. 16.

19. Brockopp, Gene W. *Review of Research on Multi-modal Sensory Stimulation with Clinical Implication and Research Proposals*. MS., 1984.

20. Budzynski, Thomas. "Tuning in on the Twilight Zone." *Psychology Today*, Aug 1977.

21. Budzynski, Thomas. "A Brain Lateralization Model for REST." Paper delivered at the First International Conference on REST and Self Regulation, Denver, Colorado, March 18, 1983.

22. Green, Elmer and Alyce. *Beyond Biofeedback*. New York, Delacourt. 1977.

23. Peniston, E.G., and P.J. Kulkowski. "Alpha-Theta Brainwave Training and Beta-endorphin Levels in Alcoholics." *Alcoholism* 13: 271–79. 1989.

24. Hutchison, *Megabrain Power*. New York: Hyperion, 1994. p. 31.

25. Pines, Maya. *The Brain Changers: Scientists and the New Mind Control*. New York: Harcourt Brace Jovanovich, 1973.

26. Lynch, Gary, and Michael Baudry. "The Biochemistry of Memory: A New and Specific Hypothesis." *Science* 224 (1984): 1057–63.

27. Hutchison, p. 203.

28. McAuliffe, Kathleen. "Brain Tuner." *Omni*, Jan 1983.

29. Harvey, Ruth S. "The Miracle of Electromedicine." *National Institute of Electromedical Information, Inc. Digest Bulletin*, Winter, 1985.

30. Starr, Douglas. "Brain Drugs." *Omni*, Feb 1983.

31. Lester, Henry A. "The Response to Acetylcholine." *Scientific American*, Feb 1977.

32. Flood, J.F., G.E. Smith, & A. Cherkin. "Memory Retention: Potentiation of Cholinergic Drug Combinations in Mice." *Neurobiology of Aging*, Vol. 4 #17, 1978.

33. Hutchison, p. 136.

34. Sitaram, H., H. Weingartner, J.C. Gillin. "Choline: Learning and Encoding of Low Imagery Words in Man.." *Life Sciences*, Vol. 22, 1978, pp. 1555–1560.

35. Sitaram, Gillin. "Human Serial Learning: Enhancement with Arecholine and Choline and Impairment with Scopolamine with Performance on Placebo." *Science*, Vol. 201, 1978, pp. 274-276.

36. Hutchison, p. 135.

37. Hutchison, pp. 147-148.

38. Bylinski, Gene. *Mood Control*. New York: Scribner, 1978.

39. Koob, George F., Floyd E. Bloom. "Behavior Effects of Neuropeptides: Endorphins and Vasopressin." *Annual Review of Physiology*. 1982.

40. Legros, et al. "Influences of Vasopressin on Memory and Learning." *Lancet*. Jan 7, 1978.

41. Davis, Joel. *Endorphins: New Waves in Brain Chemistry*. Garden City, New York: Dial Press, 1984.

42. Routtenberg, Aryeh. "The Reward System of the Brain." *Scientific American*. Nov 1978.

43. Hutchison, *Megabrain*. Ballantine Books: New York, p. 151

44. Weintraub, Pamela, Ed. *The Omni Interviews*. New York: Ticknor and Fields, 1984

45. Hutchison, *Megabrain*. Ballantine Books: New York p. 156

46. Stroebel, Charles. F.Q.R.: *The Quieting Reflex*. New York: Putnam, 1982.

47. Benson, Herbert. *The Relaxation Response*. New York: Morrow, 1975.

48. Prigogine, Ilya and Isabelle Stengers. *Order Out of Chaos: Man's New Dialogue With Nature*. New York: Bantam, 1984.

49. Fehmi, Lester F., and George Fritz. "Open Focus: The Attentional Foundation of Health and Well-Being." *Somatics*, Spring 1980.

APPENDIX II

⑥

Living The End

On October 15, 2001, I sent an email to everyone in the Centerpointe program for whom we had an email address, asking for questions, comments, and criticisms. I particularly wanted to know how everyone was doing in light the September 11 tragedy and to find out how Centerpointe might help. Here is what I sent:

Dear —,
   So much has been happening in the world this last month I wanted to check in with you and see how you're doing—both in general, and with the Centerpointe program. I know you started the Centerpointe program with something in mind you wanted to change, heal, or improve. I'm just checking in to see what progress you've been making and to offer to help in any way I can.
   Because we may be in for some very stressful times over the next few years, it's very important that you be able to increase your personal resiliency, inner serenity, and your threshold for what you can handle coming at you from the world. It's going to be very important that the world have as many people as possible with these qualities in the coming years, and I want you to be one of them.

Since nothing I've ever seen creates personal resiliency and inner peace faster or more completely than the Centerpointe program, I just want to make sure you're getting everything possible from the program.

Sometimes people misunderstand the program directions or what is "supposed to" happen . . . or start out using the program and don't see results as fast as they think they should . . . or life gets hectic and "unscheduled" things happen that get them off track...or for some other reason they just aren't regular in their use of the program. Sometimes people have tried so many things that didn't work that they become skeptical that anything could really deliver on the promises made. If the Centerpointe program doesn't deliver instant change, they assume it's just another one of those things that doesn't work, and they quit.

I know the Centerpointe program can and will deliver, and I want to do what I can to help you stay on track, get back on track, or improve your results. Seeing over 100,000 people use Holosync to improve their lives over the last 16 years, I know anyone who sticks with the program will have phenomenal results, and I feel bad whenever I hear of anyone not getting the results I know are possible.

So, if you'd like to send me a reply to this email, I will read it and reply to it personally. Send your questions, complaints, problems, challenges, triumphs, or any other comments you want me to see. I'll do what I can to make sure you get what you need to improve your results with the program and will otherwise do what I can to help you deal with whatever is happening.

I look forward to hearing from you.

Be well.
Bill Harris, Director

Have you ever been hit by an avalanche? For forty-six days I answered emails from the moment I got to work until I went home at 5 PM. Then, most evenings, I would return to my office and answer more until about 10 PM. I also spent a good deal of my time on the weekends answering those letters—including Thanksgiving and the entire Thanksgiving weekend! Although it was a tremendous grind, I'm very grateful to everyone who wrote, and I hope my replies were helpful. I know I learned a lot from those letters, and I want to share some of them with you so you can better understand what it's like to be a part of the Centerpointe program.

One of the first things that struck me as I read the letters is how many who wrote are living lives filled with personal trials, disasters, health problems, family dramas, accidents, breakups, financial losses, and much emotional pain. In my responses, I tried to give people practical advice on how to make life better, rather than just giving a lot of sympathy. It's not that I don't feel compassion for these people's suffering. My life, too, used to be one drama, one personal trial, after another, so I do know what that's like. But rather that just sympathizing, I think it's best to just get on with the job of eliminating what created the problems in the first place, and that's what I tried to do.

The second thing I noticed is that a huge percentage of the people who wrote are tremendously pleased with the results they are achieving with the program, and for that I am very gratified. Third, I noticed how many misconceptions people had about the program, how it works, and what is supposed to happen as you use it. That this happened at all is probably my fault, for somehow not communicating this information more clearly. My learning about these misconceptions prompted a complete re-thinking and revision of all our support materials. Before I get to samples of the many letters I received, I'd like to discuss these misconceptions.

Common Misconceptions About the Program

I received quite a few emails from people who said things such as, "I listened for three weeks and I'm still having a problem with anger and depression, so your program obviously doesn't work," or "I listened for nine days, but I kept falling asleep, so I knew it wasn't working and I stopped," or "My mind was really busy when I listened, so I obviously wasn't meditating and so I stopped." My favorite was, "You're obviously a quack and just trying to make money, so I stopped, even though I was actually beginning to feel better than I've felt for over twenty years." Thankfully, a great number of the people who confessed that they'd gotten off-track in using the program also professed a desire to give it another go and used my original letter as a motivation to resume the program.

Here are the major misconceptions I found:

1. *Misconception:* If you're falling asleep while listening, the meditation is probably not working.
   Fact: Almost everyone falls asleep while using Holosync, especially in the beginning, and *everything* that happens when listening is just what needed to happen, including falling asleep. Holosync works even if you nod out while listening.

2. *Misconception:* If your mind is busy, you're not meditating properly, and the program isn't working.
   Fact: A busy mind is actually a sign that a lot of stresses are being brought to the surface and released. The times when you feel uncomfortable in some way or are having lots of thoughts while meditating are often your most productive meditations in terms of releasing stresses in the nervous system and pushing against your personal threshold for what you can handle. Though these meditations don't feel as good as those where you enter a deep, trance-like state, you really are meditating just as deeply when it feels uncomfortable as you are in those times when it *feels* deep.

3. *Misconception:* If you cannot focus while listening, you're not meditating and it isn't working.
   Fact: In traditional meditation you must focus to create the brain wave patterns of meditation, and if you don't continually pull yourself back to your point of focus when you're distracted by such things as thoughts, noises, or physical sensations, you aren't meditating. With Holosync, however, the technology creates the brain wave patterns of meditation, so you *do not* have to focus. For this reason, it's okay for your mind to do whatever it wants to do.

4. *Misconception:* If you don't see results in a few weeks, a few months, sometimes even within a few days, it's not working.
   Fact: There's no magic wand. The program *will work* over time,

but it does take time. We live in an instant-gratification society, but there is no "30-day miracle" that will solve all your problems in a few weeks or months. The Centerpointe program greatly accelerates change, but it still takes time to work. We do understand that many people who have come to us have been disappointed by other approaches to personal growth. We just ask that they be patient and give the program time to work.

5. *Misconception:* If you stop using the program for a while, for whatever reason, you have to start over again at the beginning. *Fact:* This is not true. If you stop (and I hope you don't), just pick up where you left off. The effects are permanent, and do not fade if you stop.

6. *Misconception:* If life gets stressful, that's a good reason to stop listening ("I'm waiting for my life to calm down."). *Fact:* Your life is not calm because your threshold for what you can handle is too low, and it's counter-productive to forgo using the very tool that raises that threshold. Those who wait for life to be just right before taking action, generally end up never taking action.

7. *Misconception:* If a certain unpleasant experience happened when you meditated sitting up, or in the morning, or after having a beer, or when you had a cold, or when your meditation was interrupted, or whatever, this circumstance was responsible for the experience you had. Then you don't want to risk meditating while sitting up, or in the morning, or after having a beer, or when you have a cold, or when your meditation is interrupted, ever again. *Fact:* That a certain experience during a session happened under certain circumstances is almost always a coincidence. It isn't the circumstances, or even Holosync, that creates the experience you have. Whatever experience you have comes from who you are, from something inside you.

8. *Misconception:* If you change the way you use the program, and, in effect, make up your own program, you will somehow get better results than by following the instructions we've created— even though these instructions are based on what we've learned from over 3,000,000 combined listened hours, over 17 years, by over 100,000 people. *Fact:* I've created the instructions not to thwart you, but to make

the program as effective as possible. You will get the most from the program by following the instructions. Creating your own is a good way to sabotage your chances of getting the best results.

9. *Misconception:* Speed is of the essence. The faster you work through each level of the program, the sooner you can obtain the benefits.
   Fact: Doing each level for a few weeks and then saying, "I'm ready for the next level," then using that level for a few weeks and then again saying "I'm ready for the level," is a waste of time and money. This method will *not* give you the benefits of the program. The program is not a race, and hurrying will not make it work better. In fact, you will very likely not get the results you want.

10. *Misconception:* Whatever happens when you listen is *caused* by Holosync.
    Fact: What you experience when you listen to Holosync soundtracks is caused by who you are, the contents of your unconscious mind, and your own personal predisposition to resist or not resist whatever is trying to happen. The soundtracks are stimuli, but the response comes from you and says something about your inner world at that moment, not about Holosync.

11. *Misconception:* If you are not having the experiences you read about in our literature, it must not be working.
    Fact: What happens is different for each person. For some people the program is relatively uneventful, but they still gain all the benefits. Whatever happens for each person is just what is supposed to happen for them.

12. *Misconception:* Whatever experiences you have while listening are the main reason for using the program.
    Fact: Though some experiences can be quite amazing or very pleasurable, the experiences you have while listening are not important *at all* in terms of overall long-term results. They are just the mental odds and ends of meditation. It also doesn't matter if you have *no* special or unusual experiences.

13. *Misconception:* The circumstances around you are the cause of your pain or discomfort.
    Fact: It is not what is happening to you that causes pain or discomfort, but rather your resistance to it. *Any* discomfort,

anywhere in life, and certainly in meditation, is a sign of some kind of resistance, somewhere. End the resistance and the pain ends—even if the stimulus remains.

14. *Misconception:* Discomfort must be the result of *conscious* resistance.
    Fact: Even if you desperately want change on the conscious level, there can be *a lot* of resistance on the unconscious level.

15. *Misconception:* You are likely to have the same kind of experiences at every level of the program. When you go to a new level of the program, if you do not have the same kind of experiences you had in the previous level, or it does not feel as good as it did in the previous level, it isn't working, or something is wrong.
    Fact: If you are listening to the soundtracks, regardless of what experience you're having, it's working. It cannot fail to work, any more than exercise could fail to get you in better shape and burn calories.

16. *Misconception:* You can tell subjectively what is happening, how deeply you are meditating, whether it's working, and what brain wave pattern you are in while you are listening.
    Fact: Trying to evaluate what is happening by your subjective experience does not work. Constantly evaluating what is or isn't happening is a waste of time.

Excerpts From the Letters

I wish I had the space to give you the full experience of the letters I received. What appears below is a small taste, but, hopefully, a useful one. I suppose you could see these as a long list of testimonials. They are. But they're also much more. They show the range of experiences encountered by the people who use this program. They also show how much we have in common as human beings as we struggle to improve our lives.

Because they come from all over the world, and in some cases from people for whom English is not their first language, some spellings or turns of phrase may seem unfamiliar to Americans. I've done some editing where necessary, but I've attempted to retain the sense and personality of each letter.

When I got Holosync, I realized right away the first benefit was the one hour session! Now every morning, no matter what, I put my headphones on and I meditate. Actually there are two mornings that I am really pressed for time, so I just do *The Dive* [the first half-hour]. The other 5 mornings I do both tapes.

So, do I feel blissful everyday? No. I went through a period where I was very, very antsy, and I wanted to stop the *Immersion* tape [the second half-hour], but I just let it all be and I hung in there. Then I had some wonderful weeks. I just felt great and didn't want the tapes to stop! Now I am back in that antsy feeling with a gazillion thoughts swirling in my head. My committee members are extremely active!!

Do I see changes? YES! I am calmer then I ever was. I am more willing to let things go. Things happen that I don't get crazy about, and only a short time ago I would have been pissed. I don't need to be right—even if I know I am right. You know what I mean, so and so says this, you say...no this is the way it is....they insist, and I say to myself "Ellie, how important is this?"....and I drop the issue, and I smile!

— Blessings, Ellie

I am now on level four and I just love Holosync. It has done everything it has promised it would and I am so looking forward to the next 9 levels. You know it's funny, I have 2 little girls, and there was a time when all that is going on in the world would have really upset me. Although I have the utmost sympathy for everyone who is suffering, I am still enjoying, my days are happy, and I feel, just as you say, that whatever happens is O.K. I am not frightened in the least. In fact, I have come to appreciate the joy of living and our every day little ways even more, and it makes each day brighter. No words can describe what it has done for me and my family.

— My utmost gratitude, Donna

I am . . . feeling VERY stable, which is a state I have wanted to achieve for a very long time! I really hated the feeling of being on a seesaw and I no longer feel like that. I have been through some pretty tough stuff lately, and I was able to handle it all and still run our business . . . without falling in a heap. The pressure is not over yet from all that is happening around me, and I am, in the middle of it all, holding my space and functioning in the manner I desire. I am thinking clearly and getting the things done in order of priority that need to be done.

— Regards, Sue

Sorry if I make any mistakes in the English language. It's not my mother tongue. What the Centerpointe program has done for me:
So far it has helped me build up some discipline, it has helped me to relax a little, and it helps me to cope better with stress and life in general. It has cost me some difficulty to develop the discipline to follow the program every day.
There's still one important change I haven't mentioned: I feel my heart has opened. It seems to open more and more. I become more human. More sharing of my thoughts and feelings. At least I am willing to. This is important for me because I am a shy person and I want to become more human.

— With kind regards, Frits-Jan

I noticed right away since I started meditating that I am calmer, more relaxed, more focused and many other positive benefits. This alone has inspired me to stick with the program.
My new girlfriend is getting positive results too. She notices that she is getting more in touch with her intuitive side, which is awesome! Both of us are letting whatever happens be O.K.

— Sincerely, Joe

I feel an inner peace now that I haven't felt in many years. I've become so much more aware of my surroundings and my own space in those surroundings. I don't know exactly how to explain it—I just seem to feel more a part of everything and yet I'm not IN IT. I'll work on this one—maybe next time I'll be able to express it better in words.

Something silly to share on the side: my cat has even grown fond of my nightly meditation ritual. She now runs to my bed at 10 PM every night and waits for me to come in. I turn off the lights, light a candle and incense, and then listen to my tapes. The cat just stretches out and lies there like she's meditating, too.

— Miselle

The most crucial benefit is that for many years, if tired, I would be likely to doze off—fortunately, never while driving, but in meetings or classes, at work, etc. I would try different techniques to try to stay awake, such as sucking hard candy or ice, or fidgeting, but nothing worked for more than a short while. Since I started using the tapes, I noticed almost immediately that this has almost completely ceased to be a problem, even when I'm pretty tired. It's almost like some trigger in my brain has been reset, and it's a great relief. Second, I've also noticed that although I have been under a great deal of stress at work and home the past few months, I am holding up under it much better. Finally, I've tended to be very nervous about highway driving, but recently it has not bothered me nearly so much.

— Thank you for your interest and follow-up, Jeanette

I have spent much of my life searching for peace, understanding, and God, I guess. These tapes are amazing. I have been religiously listening for a month. I perceive an increase in clarity as well as less anxiety in performing most activities.

— Thank you, Dabney

Every time I meditate, the time seems to fly, to the point that I am sitting there, thinking, "oh no, this can't be finished!" I thoroughly enjoy the progress that I am making. I have managed to complete tasks and little goals I set myself each day, and if at times something doesn't work out, I always remind myself that it is meant to happen that way. Just to observe it, acknowledge it, and then move on. Everything is meant to be how it is supposed to be. Let everything be okay.

Bill, I can't possibly thank you enough. Trust me when I say that from the bottom of my heart, you have changed my life and my way of thinking around all for the better.

—Thank you! Nicole

The Centerpointe program is just what I needed in my life. Every time I meditate I finish the meditation saying "thank you" to you and your staff for this gift. I have been going through so many changes: healing, improvement in my relationships, developing strongly the observer, realizing so many things about my habitual behaviors, dealing with a lot of emotions that were hidden within, healing a lot of wounds from my childhood, trusting the process of life, feeling that my life is unfolding with much more serenity, understanding, open heart, trust. My creativity is in total flowering.

I send you a lot of love, gratitude, and blessings. Your contribution to the world is very sacred.

— Pia

I no longer lose my "cool" when speaking with people that make me angry and I have found much inner peace. The first times I did The Dive I always came out of it in tears. I was never sure why. I haven't had any traumatic revelations, but I can certainly tell the difference. I no longer cry but I do get the chills as I am listening.

—Thanks again for checking on us, Bonnie

There's a song by Stephanie Mills in which she says, "I feel good all over." That's the only way that I can describe the way that I feel. I truly feel good all over. My life seems to be in the flow. I feel just like I had been asleep for a long period of my life. And now that I'm awake I need to play catch-up because there are certain things that I should have been doing but didn't do them because I was asleep. I could write a book on just the changes that have taken place in my life. You made a believer out of me.

— Peace, James

With the nursing of my ill husband for seven years and his subsequent death eight years ago, I have been on a roller coaster ride for some 15 years.

[After his death] I noticed, and at times still notice, a feeling of panic and physical pain arising in my sternum. That was the strongest physical symptom I had during some six years of my grief. So now I am dealing with that again and going through the gradual process of healing my grief and acknowledging that I did everything I could for him. Just writing this has brought that tightness and soreness back into my sternum. But now I don't panic about it, as I understand it. I look forward to being able to overcome it completely.

I have a desire to heal myself and find an inner peace that no one can take away from me. I love knowing that I can achieve that now, and I am very grateful to your program for that.

— Kathy

For 7 years I just kept going round in circles. I would think I understood what had happened and that I had my life back on track only to find that I would get pulled back under, into the whirlpool of emotions that always seemed just beneath the surface. And all the time, I cried. Initially, I felt quite centred when I started using the CDs. Then, I think I cried for about 8 months. That's not to say that I didn't have periods of great clarity, but at times I felt like I would be crying for the rest of my life. Recently, I seem to have let go of the need to try to solve anything. It's all past. And I can't live in the past. Today I seem to be very centred. I don't cry so much, and when I do, it's a release rather than a regret. Centerpointe has played a big part in that, and I am grateful that I found you and have been able to take part in your program

— Roberta

To say that Centerpointe has been life changing is an under-statement. I intend to complete the program because it is now not just part of my life but the very bedrock of my whole expanded spiritual life. I feel I am on the path to enlightenment with this program. With every day that passes, I realize how little I know, but how much more in tune with the universe I am.

When I think back over my experience of the program so far, I can see that I have been through the pain of letting go of old ways and habits and the establishing a whole new way of being. If I had foreseen getting where I am now, say 5 years ago, it would have been an ideal that I would never have thought possible. But now, I never look back over my time on the program and think, "If only I had started this 20 years ago." That in itself is one of the most remarkable things about the program. I simply look forward along the path, and enjoy the here and now. It seems like all of life and the universe is opening up to me. I was always there but I didn't take the time to see it. My mantra these days is "It is the Resis-tance to what is that causes all my suffering."

— Best regards, John

I can't say I had an agenda for what I wanted to achieve. I only knew I wanted to be less afraid, to be more in the world and more connected to my purpose. Overall I feel more capable of handling the difficulties that have been coming my way. I was diagnosed with breast cancer two years ago. Financially things are extremely difficult, my mother has been diagnosed with Alzheimer's and I have moved her to be closer to me. Friends and family have been diagnosed with incurable diseases and my adult children are angry with each other. But I feel centered. It's quite unbelievable, but it's true. I feel much more in the moment. I have been viewing the recent [9/11] events as an opportunity for me to get clear—on what I value, why I need not fear anything and my love for human kind.

—With much gratitude, Joan

I find I am able now to detach and observe myself doing and be the witness. I am also able to remain peaceful and centred long after I would have crumbled. I can be objective about my suffering and consciously choose not to continue but to choose joy and peace instead. This is a real change for me.

I especially value the regular notes you send and knowing the Hotline is there. Sort of like a crash helmet. I hope I never need it, but knowing I have it gives me a sense of security in this anything-but-secure world. I have found I am more philosophical about recent world events knowing there are no victims and there is much I can do, just by becoming the Peace I want to see the world enjoy. Thank you and Blessings.

— Kim

I realize that I'm only at the start of the program but I've noticed a lot of changes even in that time. For example:
- increased intuition
- lucid dreaming
- bursts of creativity
- increased awareness
- more choice in my responses
- better management of my attention
- a clearer sense of purpose

One of my favourite outcomes are those unpredictable moments when I find myself looking at the world through new eyes, where old scenes have new life, colours become brighter, and everything seems clearer. This is typically accompanied with an overwhelming sense of awe and appreciation.

— With love, Tony

I believe I am doing well with the program. It is healing to me. I have handled some stressful situations without using some of my mind numbing techniques that I have used in the past. I have seen a big change in my eating habits, and this is a good thing. I have been diagnosed with adult-onset diabetes, and I have tried hard for a while to treat it with diet and exercise. I feel now that I really want to do these things for myself and before I did them because I felt I had to. There was some kind of mental block there that seems to have been lifted or at least diminished.

— Thanks so much, Vicki

Focusing, centering, less reactive behaviour. These are the miracles, those everyday miracles, that come, slowly and steadily, since I have been using your program. I've always been a bit skeptical about those who profess instant cures or solutions (which by the way you did not), and the slow, steady and consistent change has been noticeable, not only to me, but to those around me as well.

Here's an example: dealing with lawyers, with a father who I have had a very rocky relationship over the years, with a very suspicious step-sister, and with an aversion of my own to confrontational situations. Last Friday, all these elements came together, and when all was said and done, I was calm, consistent, and focused through a meeting that could have ended in a very different flavour (i.e. me being kicked out of my father's house). Instead we hugged and cried and decided to work together, even if we disagreed on any number of points.

171

When I walked from my Dad's house, I was calm! Now for me, that's nothing short of a miracle. You've made a skeptical, untrusting doubter into a believer.

—Tom

I have been diagnosed with Post Traumatic Stress Disorder and since starting the program have had some wonderful, symptom free days—feeling happy, hopeful, rested, and hungry. Issues are surfacing rapidly, and I have been taking breaks from listening when they come too fast. Since the September 11th bombing, a lot of feelings of dread, anxiety over the unpredictability of retaliation, muscle tenseness, problems sleeping, etc. have resurfaced (all very old and familiar feelings), but this time I feel more detached from it and seem to be taking it less personally, being kinder to myself in allowing more sleep and relaxing activities.

—Thanks again for your dedication to this program, Janet

I started using the program when my husband had heart bypass surgery. It helped keep me be calm (or at least as much as I could be) during that time. Since then, I use the program regularly and find it helpful. I had meditated before but knew that I would have difficulty even focusing on my breath during stressful times. So I thought the program would help create the meditative experience even if I couldn't focus on the breath. Anyway, it helps me be more calm and right now, that's OK. I have some health problems myself—chronic pain. When I use the program I have less pain for a while.

— My best to you at Centerpointe, Pat

I've found over the past 6 months, my relationship with people is much, much better. I'm not as nervous as I used to be and I don't have as many negative feelings. I find that I can stand up for myself much more and am more enthusiastic in general with life.

—Thanks, Lillian

Since the start of the program there have been some startling developments in my life, particularly in the relationship area. My partner of 19 years, Sue, also began listening to the CDs each day. We have resolved problems that have dogged our relationship for the last 12 years, and this has been done without anger or rancour of any kind. We had simply accepted that there were certain aspects of the relationship that would never change and that would continue to cause both of us pain and anguish. We found that we were not locked into stereotypical situations normally offered as a solution. Our current relationship is very different to anything we may have considered earlier.

Just the act of observation has changed my habitual response on many such occasions. There is one consequence of the program that I regard as of paramount importance to me: I have discovered what really makes me happy. The real significance of the discovery was the fact that what really gave me pleasure and what I really regard as important—and is in fact my life's purpose—is not of earth-changing consequence and did not require a choir of angels to announce the fact. It is actually very simple and very personal. I am freed of the need to feel that I have to have an important function to fulfill before I can achieve any meaningful pleasure in life. Wow!

— Regards, Alan

When I first saw the ad for your program I was at a stage in my life when I wasn't sure how I would get through each day. My husband has Parkinson's disease, and my mother, 84, who lives with us, has dementia and associated depression, and I was so

173

stressed out that I was at the stage of getting into the car and just taking off. Your program has been a lifesaver for me. I am coping with the stress so much better. I'm not as angry or quick to snap as before. Now I tend to let the little things, that used to seem major, slide past and not react to them. I am learning, slowly, to look after myself and not to try to be everything for everybody. I am becoming my own person, slowly.

— Regards, Carol

Two days ago my mother died in her sleep, not unexpectedly, after years of illness. My dad is in a hospice house, a place where they care for terminal cancer patients and is expected to die at any moment. I know that the Centerpointe CDs have been instrumental in keeping me calm, at peace, and centered during these times, and upon reflection occasioned by the receipt of your letter, I would also like to add that recently I have noticed significant improvement in what I call my running commentary memory recall ability. Do you know what I mean? I don't need to grope for the right words or search so hard for immediately necessary information.

—Thank you, D.

I've been clawing my way through an extremely difficult transition period for several years now—every identity I had either slipped away or was stripped away (horrific divorce, some friends died, others moved away, children went off to college, I lost my job, I lost my home, my mother died, etc, etc). All pretty normal life "stuff," but the cumulative effect left me quaking.

I'd already spent years and thousand of dollars doing all levels of another program, and they are very powerful—I'd also read all the self-help stuff. I'd done journals and workshops and counseling and I'd made progress, but there were just some very destructive patterns that I wasn't able to unchain.

Then something shifted. I ordered the Centerpointe Program with a surprising inner assurance, and I have been listening to the

174

Dive and Immersion CD a minimum of 2x per day—morning and evening—ever since (often a few more times during the day while I do some yoga poses. The CD calms my mind while the yoga calms my body)! I am making quantum leaps forward in the dislodgement of my "old pattern" thinking. Chaos precedes Creation.

— Love and laughter and deep peaceful joy, Brie

For about two years I have endured chronic pain from osteoar-thritis in one knee, the emotional trauma that followed from not being able to continue being an athlete, and the weight gain that followed. In listening to Level I, I have found my pain tolerance has risen. I just sustained an injury to my other knee and have found my ability to emotionally deal with it to be much higher than I anticipated. I am not as angry or upset as I thought I would be.

— All my best to you, Anna

I look forward to my meditations, find them quite relaxing, and have begun getting up at 5 am, get a cup of coffee, watch some news, and then meditate for an hour at the beginning of the day. This seems to be the schedule that suits me best. I've also begun to learn the art of witnessing, and many times have found myself starting to react the old way and stopped myself, quickly analyzed where I was going, and changed direction with a new, more resilient, better reaction to a difficult situation. I'm taking an active part in making myself become a better person, and it is a very empowering feeling.

I've also become a more compassionate person and have become able to accept that which others have to offer without being judgmental or looking down on those with less self-aware-ness. I have transformed myself from a "glass is half empty" person to a "glass is half full" person. I still have limited patience with my mother, but I hope with more time that, too will improve (Please tell me you can guarantee it!)

— Stay safe and well, Sid

Before I found Holosync, I was just beginning to be involved in a project (long-term, big). Two months into the project I was distressed that it was not taking off. I dreaded project meetings. I was jittery, inarticulate, unimpressive. Sometimes, I tried too hard and the strain showed.

Suddenly, two months into Holosync, things began to happen. My pieces were cleared...got published and got "notable" public response. I got unsolicited calls from the client: "Your promotional activities were so successful we could hardly cope with the queries." Today, meeting with the client is almost a pleasure.

In my personal life, a problematic son is suddenly exhibiting progress. For years, he was unable to hold down a job for more than two months at a time. Immediately after I began Holosync almost four months ago, he found one, and he's still at it. He's happier and more self-confident now than he has ever been.

— All best, Annaho

I look forward to my hour in the morning—the time passes so quickly, and since I am on this program I require much less sleep, and go to bed at night still feeling energized. That is what has amazed me. This program has given me longer days to accomplish the things I love doing. It's like getting a 30-hour day.

Incidentally, for your record, I am fast approaching my 77th birthday, and life has never looked so good!

— Love and light, Darlene

If I look back at just the period I passed recently, [I notice] how many things in my complicated life I am really starting to resolve—problems that have TORMENTED me for about 20 years!! I've gotten my very best friend involved. We are talking up a storm resolving our problems and GROWING and getting our lives together. It hasn't been an easy ride, though. This old stuff is hard to "digest," but to tell you the truth, I'm coming out much more easily and painlessly than I would have imagined, so this is another plus. I'm sure that my future, even though hard times will still come about, will be bright and happy in ways I cannot imagine now!

— Warmest regards, Annamaria

I had a bike accident during the summer and had casts on two hands, but I was amazed at how well I took the disaster and felt really "up" and accepted what had happened as just one of those every day incidents. I do believe without having those CDs I would have been upset and depressed.

— Margaret

In my younger days I ran and ran for Kenya. Now that I am much older I need to lose weight. After listening to your tapes I made a conscious decision that I had to do something about this weight because my body is, after all, the temple of my soul. I also notice, when I do meditate, the strength that comes out of it is immeasurable. There is so much extra energy and so much is accomplished during the day—more than what would have been otherwise. How is it possible when on a normal day I am worn out by 3 PM? However, on a day of meditation I can actually go straight to 11 o'clock. Amazing.

— Parin

Recently I have awakened to another level and life seems exciting again. I seem more aware of what is happening around me. I feel happier and more focused. I'm able to handle stress much better lately. I am experiencing a calm and inner strength, which I find so helpful in the workplace as well as in my personal life. Previously, I felt like a cloud was hanging over me. This went on for so long, I was beginning to wonder whether I would ever snap out of it. However, I continued to listen to Holosync and just like you said, the old model will eventually begin to break down and a new one will emerge. My awareness is becoming more heightened as I progress through the program and I look forward to the future when I will be even more awake and aware.

— God Bless you Bill, Clayton

In the months I have been faithfully listening to the tapes, that which is truly me has not changed, but many things that were part of my "ego"—social mechanisms, automatic responses, detrimental behavior, confusions, listlessness, ad infinitum (hopefully not)— have begun to disappear at an alarming rate. I went from drinking alcohol for years as my favorite hobby, to not drinking at all. I am attending AA meetings and have finally realized I am not my own higher power, only a part of it. I had tried to quit drinking numerous times. After a month and a half of Centerpointe, I finally simply quit, and have no desire to drink at all even though I've recently gone through some very stressful times, which I easily handled. Things are serendipitous and life has become beautiful for me, my wife, and my daughter. Thank you from the bottom of my spirit.

— Ryan

I wanted to mention that in having used this meditation, I have found that it is much easier to LOVE everyone around me. I haven't really heard this coming through the newsletters but I believe the gist is there. It is much easier just being me. I am laughing and finding things more humorous. My serious self is loosening up. I like the calming affect that this meditation has over me. While using Holosync you are naturally bumping up your vibration to becoming a better person and, in effect, will make the world a better place to live in.

— Bettyann

I think your program is awesome for me. After 12 years of panic attacks, I would go to work (I am a Hairstylist for 27 years) and come home. Going into a grocery store would be too much. I am now going to the store without dragging one of my family members with me, just in case I freak out in the store. I can now go into a shopping mall as long as it has good ventilation. I still have trouble with stuffy overcrowded rooms. And every day is easier. I just spent Friday night and Saturday with a group of strangers in a church I have not attended, to do a workshop I really wanted to do. And did it! I went there to learn paper cutting, and did. The teacher of the class is gifted and I received her gift. There were some people there I would have just left instead of dealing with. But I went there to learn the craft of paper cutting, not to worry if I would fit in. Thanks to Holosync and you, Bill. I am building a new life, not such a reactive one.

— Sincerely, Teri

I'm in the military and am stationed overseas now. When you say that the future is stressful, you're right! I have found with the program that I'm more focused and calmer during stressful times (which is just about every day, multiple times a day). Because I am a professional warrior, the program is invaluable in helping me maintain a sense of balance.

I guess what I'm really getting at is that the program is compatible with military life and has increased my performance in and out of the field.

— Van

I was one of those people who did not feel much of anything for the first few months of meditating [with Holosync]. I have been faithful in my daily practice (more so than with anything that I have ever done), having missed only occasional days due to a change in routine. After about four months, I noticed that I felt clearer, more focused, more competent in my job and, generally, more centered.

All of the things that you said might happen, I finally began to feel. I still feel a fair amount of anxiety during meditation, which I am curious about because it is not about anything in particular. My thoughts during meditation are random and mundane. I gave up thinking that I should be having deep, spiritual insights. I just don't, and I'm letting that be ok.

I have been as faithful as possible with listening to my discs and have felt much better since I started. There have undoubtedly been changes, but feeling very natural and gradual. When talking to a friend of long acquaintance, (after not being in contact for a couple of months), after we had talked for a while, she asked what had changed. To her, I sounded different and she's "relating to me on a whole different level." That's what I call progress.

It's as if life for me has turned into one heck-of-a ride and I'm holding on fast so I don't miss a thing! For sure, not all days are terrific, but the ones that aren't are much easier to cope with. More often than not, the good is gleaned from even the most dire-appearing circumstance.

— Thanks again, Paul

I have been going through massive change in my life, such as a second marriage breakup, which is nevertheless very empowering. I am coping very well with the pain and anger that I need in order to let go of this addictive relationship, and your Holosync tapes help a great deal. I have read all your literature, and although I am really quite skeptical by nature, I have come to trust you very deeply.

— With my very best wishes and my sincerest thanks, Margaret

Traumas and incidents in my daily life would come through during my meditation as tears or anger. Family incidents would send me into an emotional sobbing, crying state when I meditated. After the meditation I would feel drained but elated at the same time. I felt energy releasing on and around my head, first on one

180

side and then on the other during the meditation on several occasions. I have been floating and lost body awareness. This can happen for a short time at most of my sessions. I am now at the stage where I can sit through a session without moving, calmly, no fidgeting, scratching, or emotional outbursts. I am aware of emotional thoughts and incidents but just let them go. I can observe and move on. I feel good about myself for the first time for a long time. I don't seem to have a lot of energy, but I do feel a little lift in my spirits. I even think more kindly of people.

I am a 58-year-old grandmother and I seem to see most things in a different perspective (except my sons-in-law, of course; they're still not good enough for my daughters—just joking). I like the different feeling, when it happens, more and more.

— In faith and truth, Anne

A few days ago, I had a beautiful experience. I was at a restaurant eating with my brothers and sisters (we are 6) and suddenly a tree from across the street fell toward the restaurant and ended very close to our table, making terrible noises as it went down, and catching the electric wires causing an explosion and a lot of "lights" jumping out of it. I remember being aware of everything, each second of the experience—aware of my feelings, of my brothers, and my surroundings. And, I remained calm and centered all the time. This experience told me I am really changing for the best.

—Thank you for everything, Maricarmen

For the last 3 years, I have been going through the process of divorce, and emotionally I felt that it put me in a loop I simply couldn't get out of. I wasn't myself. In fact I could say I wasn't in touch with my Self. I wanted my Self back, and I got it:
• Ability to feel things again (in an intuitive, almost psychic sense)
• Ability to see the big picture again (holistic view, versus event by event)

- Being happy just because I realize I am blessed (as we all are)
- Knowing that what I am seeing outside is a result of my beliefs inside (limitations AND possibilities)
- Etc, and more!

Since using the Centerpointe program, everything has taken on new, positive meaning. Not that it was ever so bad before, just that, well, it's almost like I can see the Light now. It's positive, and it's beautiful.

— Kind regards, Steve

I am more powerful in the area of making and sticking to good decisions for myself: eating less junk food, exercising more regularly, and choosing activities which give me a sense of connection to the joy in life. I have a very good relationship with myself. My social life is improving. I am more able to take on an observer role and notice that others are often as uncertain as I am, or as likely to feel they said or did the wrong thing. Before, I would cut others more slack than I would myself. I am increasingly able to be more compassionate with myself and others, and conversely, also be more discerning about my own boundaries.

— Regards, Cynthia

I've been in the program for 7 to 8 years now, the past two years with Purification level 3 [the eighth level of the program]. This is the longest I've stayed on a level but I've learned over the years to recognize when I'm done with a level and I haven't yet felt that feeling. It still works each day, one day at a time. I find that as I get closer to the final levels, I don't want the program to end, whereas in the first levels, I couldn't wait to move on (thinking it was how I measured my progress), I now feel free to take as long as possible on each level.

I have also been hit by the economic downturn (I had an internet business which tanked in the past year) yet I find myself unusually calm about my financial future. I sense that things will turn out how they are supposed to go if I just keep putting forth my best effort and trusting the universe to make up the difference.

I wouldn't trade my life with anyone because I feel completely free of stifling belief systems and limiting mind programs. Thanks for discovering and creating such an incredible tool that has helped me reach this state of acceptance, peace, fun, joy, pain, sorrow, and serenity. What more could one ask for in life?

— Best Wishes, Randy

God Bless you for your program. You are literally saving my life. I seldom have self-destructive thoughts anymore. My heartburn problem is gone! I can eat onions again! I seldom if ever binge on cookies anymore. I recognize that no one makes me feel psychological pain and no one makes me suffer. Those are my choices. I live for the day that I can feel like I did when I was 8 years old, had just finished playing whiffle ball with a friend, and was lying on my back on the school's lawn looking up at a deep blue sky with a few puffy white clouds in it. The drone of a small plane sounded in the distance and was almost hypnotic. I've never felt as peaceful as I did that moment on that day. I am confident that when I reach the end of the Centerpointe journey, I'll feel that way again.

— Thanks for caring, Mark

I've been on a pretty even keel over a stressful year of being laid off and scrambling for freelance work anywhere I can find it. I attribute the program to keeping that calm. I do think the program is the best self-help program I've participated in, and I've done a lot of them. I think your theory of raising the 'trigger' level for dysfunctional thoughts and behavior is right on target. Thanks for making a great program!

— Black

I normally scoff at most of the ads I see for personal growth tools but in the ad I saw for the Awakening Prologue the rationales were logical and plausible. I knew this just may be something. The reports were excellent. I started the program and my life has changed.

—Thank you so much, Dawn

I have just ordered the second level, and I am truly more than pleased with the results. Situations and people who used to have the ability to ruin my day, I can now just blow off. At night, when trying to go to sleep, my mind would go on "engine run on." Now I am simply able to fall asleep.

I am definitely an "energy pusher" variety. But that is not at all bad. I have tried to direct the energy into things I really should have done some time ago. This summer, I managed to get three rooms painted, and get the woodwork put up. I also lost 10 pounds that needed to be lost, without making any efforts. The foods that I now crave are of a healthier variety. I am about to pass the five year mark of cancer recovery, and believe a great deal is due to the fact that Holosync has enabled me to change my entire attitude and method of dealing with life and its problems.

I do not expect the problems to disappear, simply that I will be able to handle them better.

I am hearing very little these days from the inner critic. In fact, I do believe that she is so "wowed" by the results from the Holosync program, that she is taking up a new role as "the observer."

Thank you so much for your dedication to this, your life's work. I believe that you saved one right here.

— Rosemarie

Thank you so much for your letter. I've appreciated the support letters and the personal care integrated into your program. Your letters have emphasized that we should accept whatever is happening during the program and not to resist and I think that has been the most helpful advice for me. I feel that my threshold for stress has increased markedly and I am sleeping better than I have in over ten years. I am a 55 year old, six year graduate student at the University of California, Riverside, and have been under considerable stress for some time as I move through my Ph.D. program. I have tried many other programs and your program has had a continuous effect on many aspects of my life, however, the main purpose of purchasing your program was to break through a stalemate between myself and moving forward in my academic program. I am becoming more accepting of the stress of my program and am able to work towards my goal in spite of various deadlines. I continue to balk at times but am able to accept the detour and continue to work towards progress. I am in the final phase of my specialty exam and then will prepare for my orals. Your program has permitted my continued emotional growth in dealing with issues of success.

— Thank you again for a wonderful addition to my life, Pam

A few things I have noticed:
1. Death doesn't worry me.
2. I'm a lot more aware. Of everything inside and out I mean. A guy cuts me off when I'm driving. When I was younger I would have had steam coming out of my ears. But now it's odd—I see it coming! I am aware of the surge in blood pressure, guts tightening, demonic thoughts, etc , as if I were a detached observer. And here's something even more odd. I CAN CHOOSE to react or not react, i.e., if I wish, I can be angry or calm. It's a strange feeling. I am more aware in and out.

— Best wishes, Dave

Please rest assured, Mr. Harris, that I'm getting no less than amazing results from the meditation CD's. I always look forward to meditating with them every evening. I'm more calm and self-confident than I've ever been, and am much more aware of myself than I used to be.

The most incredible turning point in my life took place this year when I was diagnosed with cancer. Since I've always had perfect health, I really had to look carefully at how I was really feeling inside, and step out of what was not working for me. Your organization came to my attention at the exact time that I was ready for it. I am very thankful for the work that you have done—you obviously care a lot about people and the world at large.

I thank God for you and this great movement. Hope to meet you at a retreat sometime!

— Paulette

It's nice to hear from you. We haven't talked since the retreat I was on a number of years ago. Occasionally I talk with the people who work with you, ordering a product or a new level.

The answer to your question is that I'm doing well. I started with the Centerpointe program because my life was in serious trouble. I had every expectation that things would change if I let them, and that eventually I would notice how they were changing. The support letters you sent out the first few months of the program were helpful, and I never fell into the trap of having specific expectations of milestones or markers or particular outcomes. I just continued to listen, working through the levels as they came. Some took longer than others (or rather, I took longer with some levels than with others). I took seriously the advice that if I started feeling seriously overwhelmed, I might benefit from backing off a little. I read some Ilya Prigogine, and that kept me distracted for a while. Mostly I just kept on.

And life is pretty good for me. I was able to cope with several years that were difficult on both a personal and professional level. Having made it through the wilderness years, I now find myself in a good space, working with lots of really good people.

I have begun to be able to remember that every difficult situation I find myself in and every difficult person I encounter are there to teach me to deal effectively with another aspect of the universe and myself. And when I witness those encounters with curiosity, I remain in a good space and begin to learn.

Is all that due to the Centerpointe program? I think it mostly is.

So thanks. You've given me the tools and opportunity to do wonderful things with my life.

I like to recommend the program to other people when they're curious. My latest tool is to forward a copy of your 9 Principles and give them the web address. The 9 Principles are very well done. I like to review it now and again.

Thanks to you and to the Centerpointe staff for your continuing contributions to the possibility of serenity for so many people.

— Brian

Actually, I am delighted with my progress. I have to say that the technology certainly delivers what you say it will. I have noticed incredible, objectively verifiable growth over the time I have been using it. Thanks also for the article on the nine principles. It is very enlightened, and profoundly helpful.

I am so grateful for your products and your wisdom. Keep up the fantastic work!

— Anna

Thank you for your E-mail. I love the programme and am getting so much out of it that I have recommended it to friends. In any case, I'd like to add my voice to those that say how wonderful this programme has been for them. People at work are commenting on how much younger I'm looking and want to know what diet I'm following, because I seem to have such a zest for life now! I find I am much calmer and am able to step back a little and observe what's happening rather than simply react to a situation. As I teach 16-17 year olds who have special educational needs my job is very stressful —or at least it used to be. I now find I'm much more able to deal with situations effectively without becoming stressed.

— I hope this finds you in the best of health, Chris

For me, the program works in subtle, unexpected ways. There is no question in my mind that using the program on a regular basis has affected the way that I react to such things as the Trade Towers incident. I am certainly not going to claim that I have been immune from having an emotional reaction to the recent events. I will say though that, unlike my former self, I am much more easily able to detach from the reaction and become the watcher. I find that I can step aside from my stuff, dissect what is going on and dig for the root of the reaction in a way that previously I could not imagine. I anticipate that with more soundtrack time I will increasingly remain balanced when confronted with events and situations that formerly would have automatically upset my apple cart. From the balanced state you can always chose how you WANT to react, if at all!

— Ralph

What a treat to get an email from you. I have just started *Awakening Level 2.* I have missed only about 4 days in the 9 months I have been involved in your program. I certainly plan to complete the program, and only worry that after I finish Flowering 4, I will be wanting more. I cannot imagine my life without these daily meditations.

I have been meditating for 12 years (Vipassana meditation) and practice mindfulness constantly throughout my day and night. Centerpointe has enhanced my "ordinary" meditations. I see daily changes in myself—insights, weight loss, improved sense of belonging in the world, more tolerance of overwhelm. I am still very much a beginner and much of my process includes pain and vulnerability —yet it all seems in a good cause—my own in-creased wholeness and increased capacity to take in the whole-ness of the world.

Thank you so much for discovering this tool and for sharing it with us. You have truly offered a great service.

—Take care. These are hard times, Kathy

I am working alone so I have read your materials carefully more than once and found them to be quite helpful. They are consistent with spiritual truths I have explored in other ways though written in your own style which is clear and direct. From the very beginning I have been able to trust you. Many of the things you write about are true for me.

I've had a steady stream of insights about my unconscious thought patterns since beginning the program. I am less attached to outcomes and more inclined to accept things (including myself) as they are. The increase in my self acceptance is a huge gift.

Finally, I want most to tell you how deeply grateful I am for what you are doing. Just as you say, I've tried lots of different approaches with mixed or temporary success. I can't thank you enough for something that really works, that I can do on my own in my complicated life. Self-empowerment brings its own rewards. Thank you, thank you, thank you.

— Sincerely, Diana

Glossary

ⓖ

Alpha brain wave pattern: Electrical patterns in the brain resonating between 8 and 12.9 Hz (cycles per second) associated with relaxation, learning, meditation, pre-sleep or pre-waking drowsiness, introspection.

Beat pattern: An interference pattern created when two tones are combined, either in the air, or inside the brain. When beat patterns are created in the brain using Holosync® audio technology, they tend to entrain the electrical patterns across the entire brain to that frequency, changing the state of the listener.

Beta brain wave pattern: Electrical patterns in the brain resonating between 13 and 100+ Hz (cycles per second), associated with alertness, arousal, and cognition. In the higher end of the range, they are associated with anxiety, uneasiness, distress, and "fight or flight" responses.

Bifurcation point: The point at which an open system has reached a point of maximum chaos, and either ceases to exist as a viable system or reorganizes at a higher, more functional level.

Binaural beat: A beat pattern created by the interference pattern of two separate sound waves, equal to the difference in frequency of the two sound waves.

Brain lateralization: A condition in which one of the two hemispheres of the brain is dominant over the other.

Brain synchronization: A condition in which both brain hemispheres produce strong brain waves of a single, coherent rhythm. Often associated with deep meditation or intense creativity.

Brain wave patterns: A measure of the rhythm of electrical patterns in the brain; usually divided into four groups, beta (13 to 100+ Hz), alpha (8 to 12.9 Hz), theta (4 to 7.9 Hz) and delta, (.1 to 3.9 Hz). Certain states and mental abilities, and in some cases the production of certain hormones and neurochemicals, have been associated with each brain wave pattern.

Chaos: A condition of increased randomness, disorder, or entropy. In open systems, if the chaos reaches a certain point, the system has the possibility of reorganizing at a higher level of functioning

Carrier frequency: The lower of the two tones in a binaural beat pattern. Lowering the carrier frequency increases the effect on the brain of a binaural beat stimulus.

Complex system: A system that constantly exchanges energy and matter with the outside environment and which can constantly adjust to environmental conditions. Complex systems maintain their level of complexity through their ability to dissipate chaos, or randomness, to their environment.

Conscious: A state of being aware, in each moment, of everything that is combining to create the circumstances of the present moment, in all its relationships and connections.

Closed system: A system that does not exchange energy and matter with its environment, and therefore cannot adjust to changing environmental conditions, or whose ability to do so is very limited.

Delta brain wave pattern: Electrical patterns in the brain resonating in the range between 0.1 and 3.9 Hz (cycles per second), associated with dreamless sleep, autonomic physical and nervous system processes, and the collective unconscious areas of the mind.

Duality: The idea that the world manifests due to the tension between polar opposites, such as yin and yang, good and evil, up and down, here and there, me and not-me, and so on. Seeing the universe in terms of how people and things are separate and in opposition.

Entrainment: To determine or modify the phase or periodicity of something, such as a wave form. Rhythmic vibrations often have the ability to entrain the vibratory patterns of other objects or wave forms around them. Holosync® audio technology uses certain combinations of sound patterns to entrain electrical patterns in the human brain.

Entropy: A measure of the amount of randomness, or chaos, in a system.

Electroencephalograph (EEG): A machines used to measure electrical brain wave patterns.

Expanded awareness: A state of being aware, in each moment, of everything that is happening to create the circumstances of the present moment, in all its relationships and connections; the quality of being conscious.

Felt shift: A term used by University of Chicago professor Eugene Gendlin, Ph.D., to indicate a shift in perception or experience of a certain emotional issue.

Fight or flight response: An evolutionary mechanism in mammals, during which the brain releases various neurochemicals having a wide range of effects throughout the body, mobilizing the body's energies toward fighting or fleeing a perceived threat or danger. In many emotional and mental illnesses, flight or flight is triggered when no danger is present, causing increased stress.

Four Noble Truths: In Buddhism, a four step explanation of the human condition, describing the cause of, and solution to, human suffering.

Good child: A person who responds to their environment through a set of rules they have learned, rather than responding based on the unique conditions and possible consequences of a given course of action inherent in each situation.

Holosync: An audio technology developed by Centerpointe Research Institute that, when listened to through stereo headphones, creates changes in electrical brain wave patterns and pushes the brain to reorganize at higher and more complex levels of functioning. Typical responses include a falling away of dysfunctional emotional responses, a raising of one's threshold for what one can handle from the environment, increased self-awareness, and an overall acceleration in mental, emotional, and spiritual growth.

Law of increasing entropy: The Second Law of Thermodynamics, which says that the overall amount or randomness, or entropy, in the universe is always increasing.

Map of reality: An internal conceptualization we make of who we are and what our relationship is to the rest of the world, which includes beliefs, values, language, memories, decision-making strategies, and ways of sorting and filtering information. This map of reality plays a large role in determining our results and experience of life.

Mind Mirror: A special electroencephalograph machine, developed by British researcher Maxwell Cade, that measures and displays the relative strength or amplitude of a wide spectrum of electrical brain wave patterns in each of the two brain hemispheres.

Olivary nucleus: A structure found in each hemisphere of the human brain that helps to process auditory signals. In the case of Holosync® and other binaural beat audio technologies, the olivary nucleus reconciles two slightly differing sound frequencies to create a binaural beat in the brain, to which the electrical brain wave patterns then resonate.

Open system: A system that constantly exchanges energy and matter with the outside environment and has the ability to constantly adjust itself to environmental conditions. Complex systems maintain their level of complexity through their ability to dissipate chaos, or randomness, to their environment.

Overwhelm: A condition in which a person's internal map of reality cannot handle the mental, emotional, or physical environment, often leading to dysfunctional feelings and behaviors.

Prigogine, Ilya: Russian-born Belgian physical chemist and Nobel laureate for chemistry in 1977 for work on dissipative structures, open systems that maintain, and even increase their orderliness and complexity by dissipating entropy to their environment. Centerpointe Research Institute has applied Prigogine's model of how open systems evolve and change to personal and spiritual growth.

Quantum leap: A change that, rather than being gradual or incremental, involves one state of being ending and another beginning.

Reactor: An aspect of a person that responds to situations and events based on strategies, beliefs, values, and other parts of one's internal map of reality, that are out of one's conscious awareness and which operate automatically; the opposite of responding from the perspective of the Witness.

Relaxation response: A term coined by Harvard professor Herbert Benson, M.D., to describe a response opposite to the "fight or flight" response, in which the brain releases various neurochemicals having a wide range of effects through the body, mobilizing the body's resources inward for contemplation, relaxation, or meditation. In the relaxation response, heart rate, blood pressure, and respiration decrease, muscles relax, and oxygen and blood flow to the brain increase. In addition, the predominant type of electrical activity in the brain changes from low-amplitude, rapid-frequency beta brain waves indicative of external attention to the slower, higher-amplitude, more strongly rhythmical alpha and theta waves indicative of inward attention.

Resiliency: The ability of a complex system to handle and process increasing amounts of input from the environment without becoming internally chaotic or overwhelmed; a plasticity in the ability to respond to varied and changing conditions, showing a wide ability to adapt to changes in the environment.

Resistance: The condition of not letting whatever "is" be okay, leading to various uncomfortable feelings and behaviors; attachment or addiction to things being something other than what they are, leading to emotional distress and suffering.

Theta brain wave pattern: Electrical patterns in the brain resonating in the range between 4 to 8 Hz (cycles per second), associated with dreaming sleep, hynagogic imagery, enhanced creativity, memory, integrative experiences, and deep meditation.

Threshold: The point at which further input will overwhelm the system. Each person has an upper limit of how much they can handle coming at them from their environment; when this threshold is exceeded, most people attempt to cope with the stress of being over this threshold through one or more dysfunctional feelings or behaviors. Traumatic experiences can lower this threshold, making the person more sensitive to overwhelm and more likely to exhibit dysfunctional feelings and behaviors. Holosync audio technology raises one's threshold.

Witnessing (The Witness): Watching whatever is unfolding, internally or externally, from a curious or emotionally dispassionate perspective, as if it were happening to someone else; being aware in the moment of how each situation is being created by all concerned while watching it without emotional involvement.

For More Information

⑥

Thank you for reading *Thresholds of the Mind*. I hope the ideas it contains help you to achieve deep and lasting happiness and inner peace.

For more information about the Centerpointe program, or to join, please call 800-945-2741 or 503-672-7117. Though operators able to take orders and answer most questions are available 24 hours a day, those with detailed questions about the program should call between 9:30 and 5:00 Pacific time, when our support staff will be available to take your call.

You may also write to us at:

Centerpointe Research Institute
1700 NW 167th Place, Suite 220
Beaverton, Oregon 97006

You can also find extensive information about the Centerpointe program on our web site at **www.centerpointe.com**, where you can also request a free demonstration CD or cassette, join the program online, and subscribe to our free email newsletter, *Mind Chatter.*